MY CRAZIEST ADVENTURES WITH GOD

Volume 1

MY CRAZIEST ADVENTURES WITH GOD

Volume 1

The Spiritual Journal of a Former Atheist Paramedic

PRAYING MEDIC

INKITY PRESS™

© Copyright 2014 – Praying Medic

All rights reserved. This book is protected by the copyright laws of the United States of America. No portion of this book may be stored electronically, transmitted, copied, reproduced or reprinted for commercial gain or profit without prior written permission from Inkity Press™. Permission requests may be e-mailed to **admin@inkitypress.com** or sent to the Inkity Press mailing address below. Only the use of short quotations or occasional page copying for personal or group study is allowed without written permission.

Unless otherwise noted, all scripture quotations are taken from the New King James Version®. Copyright © 1982 by Thomas Nelson, Inc. Used by permission. All rights reserved.

Inkity Press™
137 East Elliot Road, #2292, Gilbert, AZ 85234

This book and other Inkity Press titles can be found at:
InkityPress.com and PrayingMedic.com

Available from Amazon.com, CreateSpace.com, and other retail outlets.

For more information visit our website at **www.inkitypress.com**
or email us at **admin@inkitypress.com** or **admin@prayingmedic.com**

ISBN-13: 978-1503160705 (Inkity Press)
ISBN-10: 150316070X

Printed in the U.S.A.

DEDICATION

THIS BOOK IS DEDICATED TO my daughter, Kelly. Thanks for coming along with me on my adventures. I hope I inspired you to do amazing things with God. Your enthusiasm certainly inspired me.

ACKNOWLEDGMENTS

I WOULD LIKE TO THANK a group of my dedicated friends who have given greatly to me—of both their time and encouragement:

Todd Adams, David McLain, Michael King, Diana Devlin, Paul and Ginny Wilcox, Jeremy Mangerchine, and Jesse Birkey.

I must also mention a few folks who have— day in and day out—stood beside me. These are the friends who have prayed for me, commented on the articles I've written, and encouraged me:

Adam Moser, Alan St. Andrew, Amy Rohr, Amy Rubeck, Amy & George Saavedra, Angel Thomas, Anna Thiel Wingate, Anthony Murray, Beth Pierce, Bodie Harding, Bonnie Thom, Bradford Tozier, Bren Ward, Brenda Holiday Rather, Brian Warren, Bruce Raiford, Bryan Anderson, Cameo McCandless, Candace Cartier, Charles Hoover, Cherieann Riley, Chris Paynter, Christopher Wilson, Cleo Collins, Cyndi Millet, Cynthia Becerra, Dave Albanese, David Rush, Dawn Herring Fraley, Debbie Edward Lamey, Deborah Goodlove, Diane Devine, Donna Daigle, Donna Tonya Crow, Edie Reno, Eileen Brennan, Elias Schroons, Elizabeth Gosman, Gale Gibson, Glen Hartline, Holly Elini Wentz, Hosa Emanis, Huera Gonzales, Isaiah Appel, Jacqueline Lonneville, Jason MacKenzie, Jean André Roberts, Jennifer Barker, Jessica Dury, Jim Decker, Joe Muller, John Plummer, John Uthup, Johnnie Walker, Jonathan Porter, Joyce Grindstaff, Joyce Proffitt Smith, Julie Ann Joaquin, Julie Roach Cusick, Julie Whitmore, Justin McKinney, Kate Lake, Kathy Tipper Stott, Kathyrn Dudley, Katie Stuckas, Kazuko Onishi, Kellie Fitzgerald Gordley, Kimberly Manley, Laura Hammond-Van Den Handel, Laura

Harris, Lauree Jamison, Laurie Hilgers, Linda Gold, Linda Lautitzen, Lisa Palerieri Perna, Lisa Pessecow Cummings, Lisa Sandifer Conard, Lisa Smith, Lori Simmons Orlando, Lori McKinney, Lorrie Comstock, Lyn Cox, Lyn Vinson, Mark Rayner, Marna Mitchem, Martin Best, Matthew Robert Payne, Mike Shea, Mike Waddell, Mitch Liam, Nikki Dowdell Beck, Rae Ciardi, Ray Taylor, Rebecca Ridgeway, Richard & Andrea Walker, Robin Demer, Ron Porter, Ruthie Madison, Samuel Ambrose, Sandy Blakley, Sandy Rousseau, Shelagh Pratt, Shelila Thornton, Shoa Zilch, Staci Anissa Martin, Sue Hughes, Talia Girdhari, Terry Ashcraft, Terry Mengle, Todd & Tamara Engwall, Toni Imsen, Tracy Skoog Stavnitski, Troi Cockayne, Venus Tishler, Wendee Kreitzer, Wendy Lucien, and Yaojin.

I'd like to thank Rae Ciardi, Robby Butler and Sandra and Laurence Weaver for their help with reviewing the draft manuscript and suggesting changes.

I'm grateful to my editor Lydia Blain, who once again made the process of editing as painless and as fun as possible. Thanks Lydia!

Finally, I would like to thank my amazing wife. When you read the first story, you'll gain an understanding of just how important she is to me. Thanks baby, you'll always be the one for me.

~ Praying Medic

TABLE OF CONTENTS

The Scoop 11
Love at 3,000 Miles 17
Migraine Miracle 25
Set Free 29
Little Old Ladies 33
Stop Being a Sissy 37
Shadow Healing 39
Burning Pinkies 43
I've Fallen and I Can't Get Up 45
Meet Me at the Cemetery 47
Weather Report 51
A Change of Heart 53
Casey's Story 57
Broken Shoulders & Broken Hearts 61
A Sticky Subject 63
Healing My Partner 65
Electric Blues 67
Attention Walmart Shoppers 69
New Wine 73
Prophetic Hot Tub 75
The Dr. Scholl's Anointing 79
Charismatic Chiropractic 83
Praying for a Muslim 85
Crystals, Magic Spells or Jesus? 89
Casino Willys 93

Not Drunk as You Suppose	97
Higher Than Hi-Tech	99
Gold Dust	101
The Bell Ringer	107
The Waiting List	111
A Meeting with the Boss	113
Undercover Work	117
I'm Not a Stalker	119
The Wrong Rotator Cuff	121
Ambushed	123
You Came Back!	127
Chicken Strips & Wrist Immobilizers	131
How to Do Surgery in Your Sleep	133
God Loves a Girl in Uniform	135
Only Skin Deep	139
Good Cop—Bad Cop	141
Morphine or Prayer?	145
Burning in Arizona	147
Training Wreck	151
My Head is Tingling	153
Among Friends	157
When Seeing is Believing	161
Show & Tell	165
When Wells Fargo Tells You to Pray	167
Watch One, Do One, Teach One	173
My Partner Was a Door Gunner	175
A Second Chance	179

The Scoop

THE ADVENTURES IN THIS BOOK serve as a kind of back-story to my first book, *Divine Healing Made Simple*. While teaching on divine healing, I mentioned people I prayed with who were healed—using their cases to illustrate different aspects of healing and the miraculous. Now, in this book, I reveal a more intimate and detailed picture of how God worked in the lives of those people, and many others. Of course, healing stories are woven throughout this book, but I really felt it would be helpful to include some of the other things God was doing in my life as well.

During my career I've worked in just about every kind of setting imaginable. I've worked in rural areas where we ran two calls a week and in urban ghettos where we transported eighteen patients a day. I've felt the elation of bringing people back from the dead, and the sorrow of seeing life snuffed out in its youth. I've had times where it seemed like my happiness would never end and times when I was so burned out I hated everyone I transported. I was convinced that I would continue to work as a paramedic and ride the emotional roller coaster until I was old enough to retire, if an injury or a nervous breakdown didn't end my career early.

During the first 15 years of my career I went from one job to another, looking for a place where I fit in—a place where management had high standards of ethics and the call volume was manageable. But everywhere I went I saw nothing but problems, and the harder I looked for the perfect job the more dissatisfied I became. Like most people, I assumed that the problems and the dissatisfaction had external causes that were out of my control. I wouldn't entertain for a moment the idea that I might be the cause of my own problems. But by the year 2000 the real source of my problems was coming into focus.

I had been an atheist for as long as I could remember. I seldom thought about God or religion and I loathed born-again Christians. After pride and arrogance had destroyed my most important friendships, I had a dramatic encounter with Jesus in the bunkroom of a fire station. Because of it, I came to realize that the root of my problems was not external, but internal. The issues that were causing my unhappiness and discontent were things I controlled. The Holy Spirit made some big changes in how I saw others and myself. When the Spirit of God comes to dwell in the heart of man it's the most wonderful thing. But when the spirit of religion moves in, the true light and life of God are forced into hiding.

I learned about the goodness and grace of God but they were more theoretical sides of God than practical ways in which He dealt with mankind. Due to how He was portrayed by many church leaders in my circle, I saw God as an angry old man who was fed up with man's sinful living. Since I'd been taught that my heavenly Father was obsessed with man's sins and failures, I became obsessed with them too. No one could measure up to my standards of holy conduct and I became an obnoxious and judgmental person. Not surprisingly, my self-righteous attitude quickly alienated most of my friends and family.

In 2008, my new wife and I began attending a Charismatic church. The things I saw happening there stretched my understanding of God. One day a prophet named Melody Paasch came to visit our church. I sat in the pew mesmerized as she went from one person to another telling them about their gifts and talents and about God's plans for their lives. I had never witnessed the New Testament gift of prophecy in action before. I knew the people she was prophesying to and her accuracy about their lives astounded me. I had no idea that God was willing to reveal such things to us. After watching her read everyone's mail for about an hour I said in my heart, "God, if what she's doing is really from you I want to be able to do the same thing."

Melody happened to be hosting a dream interpretation workshop the following weekend. I was working, but my wife decided to attend. She came home from the workshop and told me that Melody said she could pray for anyone who wasn't having dreams. The last dream I had was more than 25 years ago, so she prayed for me to have dreams. That night God appeared to me in a dream and said He was going to show me what was wrong with my patients. He wanted me to pray for them and said that if I did, He would heal them.

At the time I didn't believe in divine healing or miracles. I'd never seen a miracle myself and I had never heard a legitimate testimony of one. My wife and I actually had a disagreement a few months earlier where she informed me that she believed healing and miracles were still happening today. I gave her all of my best arguments why they were not happening. We agreed to disagree and left it at that. Apparently God overheard our conversation, and wouldn't you know it—He took my wife's side. Filled with skepticism and fear about what people would think of me, I began the journey of learning how to pray for people to be healed.

Since I had never considered the possibility that God was able to or willing to heal people, I had no idea where to begin. I had gathered a collection of Christian books over the years, most of which I had purchased at thrift stores. None of them taught about healing or miracles and many of them taught that these things ceased thousands of years ago. One day I heard the Holy Spirit suggest that I should pay a visit to a Goodwill store that I was driving by. I parked the car and went inside. I went to the religious book section, but I didn't know what I was looking for. Scanning the shelves in desperation, I searched for some book that might help me.

Suddenly there it was—a thin book of no more than 100 pages, hidden amongst hundreds of other books. I read the title on the spine: *A Physician's Witness to the Power of Shared Prayer*. I took it from the shelf and began reading it in amazement. Here was a book written by a surgeon who actually prayed with his patients. A glimmer of hope arose in my heart. If a doctor could learn how to pray for his patients, I thought, so could a paramedic. I bought the book and took it home. The book didn't contain a lot of stories of the miraculous. But it made me realize that it wasn't all that unusual for medical professionals to pray for their patients. It also taught me that even if they aren't healed, patients are usually encouraged and grateful that a stranger offered to pray with them.

The book inspired me enough to begin a conversation with God. I confessed to Him that I was absolutely terrified at the thought of asking a patient if I could pray with them. I also admitted that I was doubtful that anyone would be healed, despite His promise that they would be. I just couldn't get my mind around the idea that I would witness miracles happening. So I made a deal with Him: "Lord" I said. "I'll pray for the patients I transport for the next month, but I expect some of them to be healed." With the courage of a three-week-old kitten, I prayed silently on each transport in whispers too muffled to hear: "Lord if it is your will, please heal this person."

A month went by and I prayed for everyone I transported. I was too afraid to ask anyone if they wanted prayer, so I never asked. I just prayed silently for all my patients and no one was healed. I felt like I had God right where I wanted Him. He said He would heal people if I prayed for them and no one was healed. I figured I had done my part, but He wasn't holding up His end of the deal. Then one night He gave me a dream where I was praying for a patient in the ambulance and they were healed. Apparently, I wasn't getting out of this so easily. In the morning I went to work and grudgingly found a patient that I thought might be willing to let me pray with them. She was a sweet little old lady and I sheepishly asked, "Would you mind if I prayed with you?"

"I'd be delighted," She replied with a smile.

I took her hand and nervously said, "Lord, if it's your will, I ask you to heal this precious child of yours in the name of Jesus." We arrived at the hospital and nothing had changed. The following day I prayed with another patient in the same way. "Lord, if it's your will to heal, I ask you to do so, but if it's not your will, I ask you to give them the strength they need to endure your refining process." Once again, there was no change in their condition. This went on for several weeks. I realized that although no one was being healed, everyone I asked was willing to let me pray.

I prayed with most of my patients over the next few months and even began praying for people in grocery stores, and restaurants but not a single person was healed on the spot. I can't tell you how many times I came home frustrated, embarrassed and just plain fed up with trying to get people healed. Yet invariably, just about the time I was ready to quit, I'd wake up from a dream where I prayed with someone who was healed. Some days the dreams were the only thing that kept me going.

One day while searching the internet for clues about how to get people healed, I found a video featuring a dreadlocked, ex-drug addict named Todd White who was going out on the streets and praying for strangers to be healed. And strangely enough, the people he prayed with testified that they were healed. I watched him with fascination, but I was equally confused. Todd was commanding pain to leave. I thought to myself, who the heck does he think he is? You can't just command pain to leave. It doesn't work that way!

The problem was that Todd was seeing people healed and I wasn't. I wanted to see people healed, but I could not for the life of me understand how you could command God to heal people. This guy who was a new believer with no credentials in theology was challenging all the information I had gathered over the years about prayer. And there were other things about Todd that challenged me. The look I saw in his eyes when he prayed with people seemed to pierce the soul of even the most hardened skeptics. His boldness took him into places few Christians would dare to go. He was doing things few of us would do. As I watched more videos I began to notice something else about him. He wasn't just healing broken legs and migraines. He was demonstrating what the love of God looks like when it wears human skin. And that's the biggest thing that was missing from my life. His relationship with God looked nothing like the lukewarm, judgmental religion I had found.

I watched all the videos I could find featuring Todd and slowly it all began to sink in. I discovered that Todd wasn't the only one doing this kind of stuff. As I searched for more information, I found other believers who were healing with power and authority in the workplace and on the streets. Hearing their stories helped me realize that this was not an impossible mission. I learned that it wasn't necessary to beg God to heal people. Jesus has already given believers the authority they need. We all have access to the Holy Spirit who is the source of power for healing. With renewed courage I climbed back into my ambulance determined to display the love and compassion of Jesus to strangers. And I knew that if I kept going I would eventually see healing.

This book chronicles my journey from skeptic to believer; from a guy who sat in a church pew every Sunday to one who sees miracles happen regularly. In these accounts, I've changed the names of my patients and some of my co-workers to protect their privacy. Through these stories, you'll see how my faith in God grew, and how miracles became normal. The fact that God has done so many miracles through the hands of a former atheist suggests that He will do them through anyone who wants to see His power and love demonstrated in their lives. The things He did through me are the same things He'll do through you, if you're willing.

Love at 3,000 Miles

ON THANKSGIVING DAY IN 1998, a woman living in a small town in Pennsylvania who had been an atheist her entire life, finally met Jesus. She had struggled and failed in her first marriage at a young age and now it was apparent that her second marriage was also dying and would end in divorce. Determined not to make the same mistakes again, she spent the next six years reading everything she could find on how to build successful relationships.

Two years later, after living most of my life as an atheist, I had a life-altering encounter with Jesus at my fire station. A few months later, while sitting beside the wood-burning stove late at night I had a difficult conversation with God. He asked me how much I loved Him.

"I love you more than anything or anyone," I said.

"What would you be willing to give up for me?"

"Everything."

"Really?" He asked.

"You can take my wife, take my kids, take my job, and take this house. You can take it all away. Just don't ever leave me."

Not long afterward I began a six year long battle to keep my paramedic license that involved two state investigations, two department investigations, and a grievance between our union and the chiefs that would cost our department over one hundred thousand dollars in legal fees. In 2003, I lost my job with the fire department. In 2005, I had an extramarital affair. That same year, I was falsely accused of domestic violence after an incident in the parking lot at my kid's school. A no-contact order was issued that prevented me from seeing my wife. It would remain in effect for three years. My wife filed for legal separation and we would eventually be divorced. Six months after my arrest, we nearly lost our home, but managed to sell it before the bank foreclosed on it. In 2006, my estranged wife moved out of state with our children. I wasn't sure if I would ever see them again. All I could do at this point was trust that God had a plan. But from my perspective, things couldn't get much worse.

Late in 2006, I was ecstatic to see my kids come back to Washington. I rented a small apartment next to the High School they wanted to attend and we were able to be together often. In 2007, I began considering the possibility of remarrying and I learned about online dating services. I spent several months going through profiles of prospective women in my area but I was disappointed with what I found. There didn't seem to be anyone within a hundred miles that I was compatible with. I expanded my search and found someone in Denver who seemed fairly compatible with me except that she wanted to have more children and I did not. I expanded my search even further to include anyone in the entire U.S., figuring maybe that perfect person was on the other side of the country.

I had a conversation with God one day where He asked me to put control of choosing my next wife in His hands. It was another uncomfortable meeting. Since I had not had much success in this area in the past, I decided to let Him choose my next wife. "Lord, I'm going to trust you. Just choose the woman who is right for me, let me know who she is, and I'll commit to loving her for the rest of my life."

One day on Christian Mingle I ran across a profile of a woman who lived in Pennsylvania. She said she met Jesus on Thanksgiving Day in 1998. Her profile picture was cute. As I read about the things she liked and disliked I didn't see a single red flag. She seemed to be the one I was looking for. The only problem was that she lived 3,000 miles away. Since my kids were in High School, moving wasn't an option for me. If we were going to be together, she would have to move to Washington. I wondered if she would be crazy enough to move all the way across the country to marry me.

God made it pretty clear to me that she was the one He wanted me to marry. So I checked the box indicating that I was interested in knowing more about her. She received a notification that someone wanted to get to know her. The dating site created a little mystery to solve by sending four photos; one of them was the man who was interested in her. She had to decide if she was interested in meeting one of them. After dismissing the other three photos, she came to mine and said, "This guy is pretty cute, I hope it's him!" After reading what I'd written about myself, she began to question my honesty, "He almost sounds too good to be true. He's either the biggest liar in the world, or he's perfect for me. It says he loves to cook—that's a big plus!" She had met some liars online in the past, as well as some very nice people. She wasn't worried about communicating with me. She knew God would reveal everything she needed to know.

We were connected through the website and she sent me an e-mail telling me a little about her life. I was pretty excited to see that she responded so quickly and I replied with a short message. I didn't want to scare her off by giving her too much information about myself, but I let her know I appreciated her quick reply. I typed out my phone number at the bottom of the message and hit send. She replied with another e-mail a few hours later. Her prompt replies told me that she was willing to invest time and attention in her relationships. I thanked her for her response and told her a little about what I had done that day. She replied a third time. I loved how interested she was in staying connected during our first day of correspondence. I wrote back: "Why don't we just skip the formalities and get married?"

We e-mailed and called each other on the phone for a few weeks. It was pretty obvious that we were crazy about each other. It looked like we had a good shot at building a long-term relationship. One day we had a serious talk about what our future held. One thing that stands in the way of a successful marriage is a lack of transparency. Out of fear that they'll suffer rejection, many people hide their past from the person they're dating. Years later when something from the past comes up (and it always does) the person you thought you knew is no longer the one you're married to. But by then it's too late. I knew that if I expected her to quit her job, leave her family and friends and move across the country to be a permanent part of my life I had to be transparent with her about my past.

So one night I told her I needed about two hours of her time, just to listen as I told her about my past. I divulged to her everything a woman would want to know about her potential husband, and I mean everything. My weaknesses, my failures, the things I did wrong in my last marriage, why I had an affair, why I was fired from my last job, my fears, my arrest, my financial problems... everything.

It was a huge risk, but I figured if she could deal with the junk from my past, she'd have no reason to fear a future with me. She wouldn't have to worry about something from my past coming up one day and surprising her. It paid off big time. She accepted me—failures and all. She said she didn't expect me to have a pristine past, but she wanted a man with a teachable spirit. She always thought of herself as a lifelong learner and wanted a man who was also able to grow and learn with her. We planned another phone call so she could tell me all about her past. Of course I accepted her, just as she had accepted me. In talking about all these things, we realized that although we had both made a lot of mistakes, we'd also learned some hard lessons along the way. We gave each other grace for past errors and sins and decided to create a future that looked nothing like our past.

I would have married her sight unseen, but she insisted we had to meet in person first. I was inspired by a message by Ravi Zacharias titled, *I, Isaac, Take Thee, Rebekah,* in which Ravi describes how his older brother (who was running his own computer consulting company in Paris at the time) allowed their parents in Canada and their aunt in Bombay to choose a wife for him. Ravi counseled his brother, warning him that an arranged marriage might not be such a good idea. His brother countered with a line of reasoning that I'll never forget: "Ravi," he said, "I am not worried about who my family will choose for my wife. I know they love me and they want what is best for me. They will choose the best person they can find. I am not worried about whether I will love the woman they choose because that is something that is completely in my control. Love is as much a question of the will as it is of the emotion. And if you will to love somebody, you can."

I told her about Ravi's message and said I would marry her without meeting her in person because I knew that love really is a choice, that God had chosen her for me, and I was ready to commit myself to her fully based on that knowledge.

She replied, "I've always loved that message from Ravi. Based on that teaching, I do understand how you could commit yourself to me before meeting me in person, but I still want you to meet me before we get married. Okay? When can you come to Pennsylvania?"

It wasn't just the fact that God picked her out for me. In the time we'd known each other I had fallen head over heels crazy in love with her. So I flew to Pennsylvania a few months later to meet her and her friends and family. She took me to work one day where I met her co-workers who were among her closest friends. One concern we both had was that people would think she was making a bad decision marrying a guy she'd only met once. There are a lot of weirdos and flakes in the online dating community and we felt like we needed to convince them that I wasn't some flake who would break her heart a few weeks after she married me.

The year after my former wife and I separated, I became addicted to the Food Network. We didn't have TV in our home while the kids were growing up, but the house I rented had cable TV. I watched every episode I could of Elmeril Lagasse, Paul Deen, Alton Brown, Rachel Ray and the other chefs who hosted shows on the Food Network. I had always liked cooking, but it wasn't until I watched these shows that I learned how to do it well.

On the Friday evening that I was in town, we held a dinner party for her friends and family so they could get to know me a little better. I decided to put my cooking knowledge on display and pulled out all the stops. I made Chicken Cordon Bleu and a side dish and an assortment of handmade chocolate truffles for dessert. Making the ganache for the truffles was an ordeal. At first it was too warm, so I put it in the refrigerator, but then it was too cold so I had to heat it up again. It took several hours to get the ganache to the right temperature. All the work was worth the effort. The truffles turned out marvelously. I'm an extrovert by nature and I'm comfortable entertaining strangers so it was easy for me to win their hearts that evening. At the end of the night, her mom said, "If you don't marry him, I will."

A few days later she drove me to the airport for my trip back to Washington. Traffic slowed to a stop on the Schuylkill expressway. Two different accidents caused enough delay that it was going to be a close call at the airport and I had to work the next day. I arrived outside the terminal and asked if my flight was departing on time. The agent said, "I'm sorry sir, but you're not going to make your flight. You must arrive at least twenty minutes before departure for all domestic flights. You won't be able to board. I'm afraid you'll have to take the next flight."

"Twenty minutes? Heck, lady I can make it to the gate in ten minutes. I really need to be on this flight."

"I'm sorry sir, but the regulations are pretty strict. I can't let you board this flight. You'll have to take the next one."

"Well, okay. When is the next flight to Seattle?"

"Tomorrow morning at six."

"Are you crazy, I can't wait that long! I have to work tomorrow."

"I'm sorry sir. That's the earliest flight we have going to Seattle."

"Fine. I guess I'll have to wait."

I called my manager to give him the news. "Hi Scott, it's me. Hey, sorry to bother you but I have some bad news. I'm sitting at the airport in Philly and they won't let me board my flight, because I got here little late. Traffic is ridiculous. The next flight they have going to Seattle is at six o'clock tomorrow morning. I can catch that flight but I won't be into work until noon."

I hung up the phone. "Well honey, I guess we'll have one more dinner together." We got in her car and she drove me back to her place. I could tell she was happy to have a little extra time with me. I was glad too. As she drove, I studied her face. I loved her nose and the reddish color of her hair. Her huge eyes flashed with deep expressions of happiness when we found a subject about which we had the same views. I tried to permanently burn a few memories of her into my mind, since I wouldn't see her again for a while after tomorrow morning. When she caught me looking at her she smiled with approval. I really was smitten by her cuteness and charm. We stopped on the way home to pick up some things for dinner. I had one more opportunity to flex my cooking muscles, so I made sweet and sour chicken with rice from scratch and we enjoyed one last night together. The next morning we made it to the airport on time. With tears streaming down her cheeks she kissed me goodbye. "I love you, mister. I'm gonna miss you so much. Call me when the plane lands."

"Don't cry baby. The next time you see me, we'll be getting married." I gave her a long hug and a kiss then got on the plane, flew back to Seattle and we began making plans for a beach wedding in the fall.

The third week of September she flew with her son to Seattle. My kids and I picked them up at the airport. She nearly jumped into my arms when I met her at baggage claim. She clenched my hand in hers on the way to the car and wouldn't let go. We piled into the rented van and drove to Cannon Beach, Oregon. We rented a couple of deluxe suites at a hotel so everyone had a room of their own. The next morning we prepared for the wedding ceremony. The sky was blue and the winds were light. The pounding surf provided a peaceful backdrop for the ceremony. It couldn't have been any better. Okay, that was a little hyperbole. It could have been a little better. It was actually a bit chilly, but this is a fairytale ending to a cool story, so let's just say it was a beautiful day for a beach wedding. In the middle of the ceremony my wonderful bride sang a song to me accompanied by her son on guitar. The tenderness of her voice and gentleness of her spirit made my eyes fill with tears.

We had a small dinner reception that night at a local restaurant with some of our family members. The next day I drove her and her son to the airport and said my goodbyes. "God did it, honey. It's hard to believe it, but we're finally married." I gave her a long hug and a kiss.

She began crying again. "I'm gonna miss you, lover-man."

"Hey, no crying, baby. The next time you see me, we'll never have to be apart again." She kissed me over and over, and then boarded the plane back to Philly. She sold her house in the middle of the worst housing market anyone could remember. Three months later I flew back to Pennsylvania to help my new wife and her son with their big move across the country to join my kids and me in Washington. We rented a moving van and drove through snow and ice on an adventure no one really wants to have when they move. After nearly eighteen hours of straight driving on the final day of the trip, we arrived at the new house we had just rented. It was time to see what God had in store for the next chapter of our lives.

Migraine Miracle

IT WAS AN UNUSUALLY HOT day in Tacoma, with the temperature near 100 degrees. My EMT partner and I were trying to find some shade for parking the ambulance in between calls. I felt dry and thirsty and I was worried about getting dehydrated, so I turned to my partner. "Hey, can you drive us to Safeway so I can get a bottle of Gatorade?" He nodded, drove us to a nearby Safeway, and parked the ambulance. I went inside. The air-conditioned store was a welcome change from the oppressive heat outside. There was a cooler full of drinks near the checkout stand so I grabbed a bottle of Gatorade and took my place in line behind a woman who was buying a bagel.

I'm not sure why, but I looked down at the floor and closed my eyes. In my mind's eye I saw an image of a middle-aged woman with blonde hair. I could clearly see the word "headaches" in white letters on a black background. I looked up and sure enough, the woman buying the bagel was the same woman I saw in my mind's eye. I felt like the Holy Spirit had just told me that the woman in front of me had migraine headaches.

She paid for her bagel and walked over toward the deli department. She was wearing a white uniform and black apron. It was then that I realized she was an employee of the store. I paid for my Gatorade and followed her to the deli. I waited until she had finished what she was doing then got her attention. "Excuse me ma'am, do you have a few minutes?"

"I sure do, how can I help you?"

"I'm here to help you get rid of those headaches."

"How did you know about my headaches?" She cupped her face in her hands and began sobbing.

"Well I was standing in line behind you at the checkout stand, and I closed my eyes and saw a picture of you in my mind with the word 'headaches.' God loves you and He wants to heal you."

As tears streamed down her cheeks she said, "You don't understand. I've had headaches for years and this morning I woke up with another one. As I was lying there in bed, I wondered if God would ever heal me of them. Then you show up and tell me that He wants to heal me. Who are you?"

"I guess I'm the guy He sent to heal you. Is it okay if I pray with you?"

"Yes, of course it is!"

She walked around the deli counter and stood in front of me. I placed my hand gently on her forehead. "In the name of Jesus, I command these headaches to leave right now. Spirit of pain I command you to leave." I looked at her nametag. "Lord, I bless your work of healing in Shelly's life." I asked how she felt.

"It's gone! It's completely gone! I can't believe it. I don't have any pain at all!"

I was dumbfounded. I had never seen anyone miraculously healed before. I had prayed for hundreds of people over the last year with no obvious fruit to show for it. I couldn't believe God actually healed someone I prayed for. I gave Shelly a hug then gave her a card to my website and asked her to keep in touch. I wanted to know if the headaches came back. I grabbed my bottle of Gatorade, said goodbye, and walked out the door into the blistering heat. Shelly wrote about this encounter on her own blog. This is her account of the story:

I had been having these extreme headaches for a while, I had gone to the doctor for them and he did not know what was causing them, I tried taking Ibuprofen and Excedrin Migraine for them, nothing worked.

The morning before work I was in my quiet time with God, trying to read Matthew 13: The Parable of the Sower. After reading it I was asking God to let his word fall on good soil (since I didn't feel like I was a good Christian.) I was sitting there and my head hurt so badly, I remembered telling God how much my head hurt and I really couldn't pray. (Never occurred to me to ask for healing as I felt like I was not worthy to ask.)

When I got to work, I grabbed some Ibuprofen out of my purse and took it, I thought I better get myself a bagel, so this stuff doesn't hurt my tummy. I was standing in line, not talking to anyone, didn't tell anyone of my headache, paid for my stuff and went back to the bakeshop.

I looked up and saw a man standing there wearing an ambulance uniform wanting to talk with me. (I just thought it was a customer who wanted to ask a question.) I ask him how can I help him? He said, "I'm here to help you get rid of your headaches." My mind started racing, thinking, what? Who told this man I had a headache? How is he going to help me? Stuff like that. Finally I ask him, "Who told you I had a headache?" And he said, "God did." He also said God showed him in [the checkout] line of my headaches, and that God loved me and wanted to get rid of my headaches. I burst into tears; that the God of the Universe would care enough about me to send some stranger over to heal me. The man also asked if he could pray with me and I said yes. So we prayed together, after we prayed he gave me this card and told me if my headaches stayed away could I please blog it.

Well everyone, it has been a week and half and no headaches! I have to praise God for loving me. Praise God for healing me, for I know when God heals He heals forever. Praise God for sending this man to heal me. And thank the man for not only listening to God but also obeying Him.

☙

I spoke with Shelly a month later at the Safeway and she hadn't had any headaches since we prayed.

Set Free

THERE ARE MANY MODELS OF personal evangelism used in the church. Some people lead a new convert in saying the sinner's prayer, some explain the four spiritual laws, or travel the "Romans road." I seldom use any of these approaches. They seem rigid and they tend to assume a great deal about the person, which may not be true. I see every encounter as unique. I prefer to let each relationship develop naturally, without a predetermined direction or goal, and without a particular method in mind unless God has given me one in advance. I prefer to let the Holy Spirit guide me in the right direction, set the pace, and determine the issues we'll discuss.

Sometimes all I do is buy my new friend a cup of coffee and interpret a dream or give them a prophetic word. With others I might answer a few questions they have about God. Sometimes it's a prayer for healing and a hug. I never really know where an encounter will lead.

When I'm with people who don't have a relationship with God, I try to approach the situation with only one thing in mind; I know God loves them and I want to give them one positive experience with Him. It may be the only one they ever have and I believe I owe that to everyone I meet. This is one such story.

We responded to a doctor's office. When our patient mentioned that she cut her wrist intentionally, the receptionist called 911. She sat in a chair crying; her tank top revealed two arms covered with large bruises and small lacerations on both wrists.

As I walked through the clinic door, the weighty presence of God that I suddenly felt made me lose my balance momentarily. The fact that

God let me feel His presence made me think He had something in mind for my patient. I was no longer the lead paramedic, but God's partner, trying to follow the lead of the Holy Spirit. An overwhelming sense of compassion came over me that I would not normally have felt. When these feelings grip me, I've learned to recognize them as the feelings God has for others. Out of these feelings, He leads me in the way He wants me to interact with them. I felt His love for our patient and I was certain He was drawing her into a relationship that she was ready for.

She poured out her heart to us over the next half hour, relaying her long battle against alcoholism and drug addiction. She said she then turned to prostitution. It was the only way she could get money for the things she needed. Her life had become one long nightmare of abuse, neglect, and addiction. "I've tried to kill myself so many times I can't count them anymore."

As I listened to her story, I tried to gauge where she was at spiritually. In my mind I ran through a list of questions: How much did she know about God? How desperate was she for change? How did she feel about Jesus? Did she have any negative church experiences? Has God been speaking to her through dreams? Did she want to be delivered of demonic oppression?

In the ambulance, I sensed a desperation that was unusual for someone in her place. Many people who become trapped in a life of drugs and prostitution resign themselves to this fate and quit looking for a way out. Her mannerisms and speech told me she would do anything to discover a new way of living. I could tell she was ready for a serious discussion about God.

"Samantha, I want to help you find a way out of all this."

"I need someone to help me. I can't do this anymore. It's killing me."

"There's only one thing that can change your life permanently."

She beat me to the punch line. "It's God, isn't it?" In her spirit, she knew what the solution was.

"Yes, it is God. He's the answer you've been looking for.

"I knew it. I just knew you were going to say that."

"Samantha, I know you've had a rough life. And maybe you've wondered why God lets things like this happen to people. I want you to know that even if you don't feel loved right now, God has loved you since the day you were born. He didn't create you to be a mess. He made you to be a beautiful and wise woman. He still wants that for you. It's always been His plan and it's never too late to make it happen.

Jesus said, 'I have come that you might have life, and life abundantly.' He wasn't lying when He said that. He really can give you a brand new life that's better than you could ever imagine."

She sat on the gurney mesmerized, taking it all in. No one had ever told her anything like this. I find it helpful to speak positively, lovingly, and authoritatively against the negative things people believe about themselves, and to declare the great things God says about them. It seems to bring freedom to people who are trapped in the enemy's lies.

"Sir... I want this new life you told me about."

It was time to lead her in a simple prayer. It wasn't a time to remind her of her sinfulness. She knew how horrible her life had been and I didn't want to make it worse. "Samantha, repeat after me. Jesus, I want the new life you promised to anyone who believes in you. I want to feel your love for me. I accept your forgiveness of my past and I want to live the new life you can give me. I want you to change me in every way. Take away my craving for drugs and alcohol and let me desire only things that are good for me." With a joyous smile she repeated everything I said. It was a special moment I'll never forget. She became very peaceful and relaxed as we transferred her to the emergency room bed. She couldn't stop thanking me for helping her.

I love the way God opens doors.

You may ask, will she live free of these things in the future? I can't say. That's a limitation I've learned to live with. My influence is small, my time with a patient is short, and I seldom know what happens after I leave them. I'm a sower of the seed, one who doesn't know what the harvest will look like.

Our nation is in a tight spot right now in regard to caring for people like my patient. A major problem in our society is the ineffectiveness of our system of mental health treatment. Most patients are in a revolving door lifestyle that never "cures" their condition. Most people with severe addictions and mental illness are unable to work and have no insurance other than what the government provides. And our government is fast running out of money.

What's the answer to our problems?

Jesus. He's always been the answer. He is the great physician. When He heals, He doesn't ask for an insurance card or a deductible. Prescription plans aren't needed, only divine appointments, and the great physician is always available. He never takes vacations.

Little Old Ladies

WE RESPONDED ON WHAT WOULD be a boring call for most paramedics: a little old lady with the flu. I informed her that there wasn't anything the hospital could do and she might be better off staying home, but my objections were overruled. She was coming with us. While loading her in the ambulance, I got her medical history. She was pretty healthy except for severe scoliosis, arthritis, and a torn meniscus in her left knee. It was the torn meniscus that got my attention.

About a month earlier, I prayed for a young woman at a grocery store who had the same problem. I saw her in a wheelchair leaving the store and asked if I could pray for her. After a few minutes of prayer she was healed. Having done it once before, I believed my little old lady would be healed, too. I told her about the healing at the store. "Would you like me to pray with you to be healed?"

"That would be wonderful!"

She had limited range of motion in her left knee with severe pain when she flexed the joint. I had her relax and placed my hand on her knee. "I command this knee to be healed in Jesus' name and I command spirits of pain to leave. What do you feel?"

"Wow, that's strange. It feels very warm."

I didn't have to ask her to flex it, she did and her jaw dropped open.

"How did you do that?" She had full range of motion with no pain. She grabbed my hands. "Thank you. Thank you, so much!"

After a short celebration in the back of the ambulance, I asked about her back.

"So you have scoliosis, right?"

"I used to be four inches taller than I am now."

"Can I pray for your back to be healed?"

"Of course you can!"

I placed my hand on her back and commanded it to be healed. She felt heat going down her back. She was on her way to having that healed, too. We talked about the goodness of God all the way to the hospital.

About an hour after dropping her off at the emergency department, we responded for another little old lady who tripped and fell. We got in the ambulance and drove to her house where we found her sprawled on the floor just inside the front door. I began to ask the usual questions.

"What happened, ma'am?"

"I'm so mad at myself." She said in a beautiful Scottish brogue. "I should have waited for help."

"Where are you from?"

"Glasgow." She said with a smile.

I instantly took a liking to her.

"Please do not touch my leg, lads. It hurts like the devil." Right on cue, a firefighter grabbed her ankle to see how badly she was injured. She let out an ear-piercing scream. I got down next to her and gave the firefighter a nudge to let him know his assessment was done and I was taking over. "Ma'am, let us help you to the gurney and we can transport you to the hospital."

"I went to the hospital early this morning. They took a peek at me but they couldn't do anything."

"You went to the hospital already? What did they tell you?"

"They didn't think it was broken and they sent me on my way."

"Did you injure your leg today or is this an injury you already had?"

"I fell and hurt myself about two months ago, lad. The doctor said I had shin splints and he told me to go to therapy, so I went just like he said but the pain kept getting worse."

"That's not supposed to happen. I mean, it might hurt for a while when you start therapy, but the pain should eventually leave as you begin to heal."

"Well lad, they misdiagnosed me. The stupid doctor never took an x-ray. I broke my leg and he didn't even know it."

We got her loaded on the gurney and wheeled her to the ambulance. I sat next to her and explained what happened on the previous transport. When I was done, I asked, "Can I pray for you?" She was so glad to have me pray she almost kissed me. I placed my hand gently on her

The Spiritual Journal of a Former Atheist Paramedic

leg and invited the Holy Spirit to join us. But before I could say a word, her hands shot up in the air.

"Praise the Lord, I'm healed!"

Her boisterous reaction caught me off guard.

"Ma'am. I'm glad you're healed, but we're going to be at the hospital soon and they're going to need you to be a little... quieter."

"Praise the Lord, and his holy name, lad... I'm healed! Thank you Jesus!"

She kept praising God, louder and louder. We dropped her off at the emergency department and she was still praising Him. I have no idea what she told them after we left and I never wanted to find out. Being a relative newbie to healing at the time, I never thought that if someone actually got healed in the ambulance it would be so... embarrassing!

As I quietly slipped out of the hospital, I whispered, "What next, Lord?"

Stop Being a Sissy

There's a whole chapter in my first book devoted to explaining what a "word of knowledge" is and how we can receive one. For those of you who are unfamiliar with this term, let me briefly explain what it is:

The word of knowledge is information given to us by the Holy Spirit revealing certain facts, which God is aware of, but we are not. It's information about a past or present situation that is true.

A word of knowledge can come in a number of different ways. Some people hear the voice of God speaking, while others might receive a word through dreams or visions. A word of knowledge for healing often presents as a sudden pain or other sensation in our body that we don't normally have. Learning to receive a word of knowledge comes by developing sensitivity to the leading of the Holy Spirit.

I was on duty one day and while getting lunch at a grocery store deli, I felt a sudden pain in the first knuckle of my middle finger. I've never had pain in my hand like this before, so I wondered if it might be a word of knowledge for healing. I asked the person closest to me if they had pain in their hand.

"Excuse me sir, this might seem like a weird question, but... you don't have pain in your hand, do you?"

The guy gave me a strange look, shook his head and walked away.

As I waited for my food, I thought maybe it was one of the people behind the counter. I waved to get the attention of the man closest to me. "Hey, you don't have a sharp pain in the back of your hand do you?"

He smiled and said no, then told me my food would be ready in a minute. I tried one more time with a woman as she walked past me.

"Excuse me, ma'am... you don't happen to have any pain in your hand do you?"

"No, why do you ask?"

"Oh, I don't know... I was just curious." She went on her way and I scanned the crowd for someone else to ask. The man behind the counter told me my food was ready. I paid for it and went back out to the ambulance.

I got in and told my EMT partner about it. "It's the weirdest thing. I suddenly developed this pain in the back of my hand. I'm sure it's a word of knowledge for someone. I asked a bunch of people in the store but no one had pain in their hand."

He gave me a puzzled look and asked, "Where's your pain?"

Pointing to the back of my hand I said, "First knuckle, middle finger."

He smiled. "I was sawing a tree branch last weekend in my back yard when the branch I was leaning on broke. My hand was jammed into the broken off branch. It's been killing me ever since. The pain was so bad it woke me up this morning. That's the exact spot where it hurts."

"So do you want to be healed or not?"

He stretched out his hand and I placed my hand over his.

"Spirit of pain I command you to leave right now in the name of Jesus. I command ligaments, tendons, bones and nerves to be healed. Okay. What do you feel?"

"Tingling... pins and needles basically."

I looked at him and smiled, knowing what God was doing. Then added my signature statement, "You're healed. Now stop being a sissy."

To someone who receives words of knowledge often, this encounter might not seem like a big deal, but I seldom receive them, so to me it was a major breakthrough. It also greatly encouraged my partner when he considered the fact that God cared enough about his pain to tell me about it so he could be healed.

Shadow Healing

ONE WINTER MORNING THERE WAS a traffic jam on my drive to work, but rather than get stressed about it, I cued up some music on my iPod and got drenched by the Holy Spirit. As drivers crept slowly toward the pile of cars that lie motionless on the freeway in the rain, I immersed myself in an incredible time of worship and thanked God for lifting me up out of the period of spiritual dryness that I had been in.

Not long after I arrived at work, my partner and I responded on a call to Northeast Tacoma. We got in our ambulance and made our way north of the downtown area through the mud-covered tide flats then turned a corner and climbed the long hill that overlooks the port. We crested the hill and a few minutes later, arrived on scene. Inside the apartment building we found the crew from engine three interviewing a middle-aged woman as she held a wad of tissue to her nose.

I looked at the lieutenant. "What's the story, morning glory?"

"Donna here has a pretty good nosebleed. We checked it when we first got on scene about ten minutes ago and she was still bleeding. It's been going on for about two hours."

"Hi Donna," I said as I introduced myself. "I have a few questions for you, if that's okay. First tell me this... have you ever had nosebleeds like this before?"

"Just once... about a year ago. My nose bled for a couple of hours and I had to go to the hospital and have it cauterized."

"I see. Are you taking any blood thinners right now?"

"Just aspirin. My doctor increased the dose a few days ago. Do you think that might be the problem?"

"Could be, but it's hard to say. You didn't take a fall or have any kind of trauma, did you?"

"No."

I had a few more minor questions to ask and I watched her carefully as we talked. She kept checking to see if there was any more blood coming from her nose, but it seemed like the bleeding had stopped.

I only have one more question for you. "Is your nose still bleeding or has it stopped?"

She held a tissue to her nose then pulled it away. "Well look at that," She said. "It seems to have stopped."

"Are you sure?"

She grabbed a new tissue from the box and held it to her nose then checked it. There was no blood on it. "I'm certain of it. I'm not bleeding anymore."

"Well that is strange, isn't it?" I asked.

"You know what's really strange about this? I think the bleeding stopped a minute or two after you got here," she said.

The lieutenant asked Donna if she wanted to go to the hospital or stay home. "I guess I'll stay home. No sense in going to the hospital if I'm not bleeding."

"You're welcome to go in and get checked if you want," the lieutenant advised her.

"No... I think I'll stay home."

He had her sign a release form then one of the firefighters tapped me on the shoulder. "Hey man, we could use your magic powers. Any chance you guys could go on our calls with us today?"

The other firefighter joined him. "That's what we need! A medic who does miracles! We can wait for him to show up and get people healed—then no one will need to be transported!"

The lieutenant looked at me. "What's your unit number again? I might request you guys to go on all our calls with us. It sure would make things a lot easier."

Even though they were joking, the guys knew there was something supernatural going on. "Really funny guys," I replied. "But I don't think dispatch will let me follow you around all day. So, L.T., do you need us to stick around or can we clear?

"Looks like your work here is done. I guess you can clear. Thanks for your help."

"All in a day's work, Lieutenant. See ya on the next one."

"I sure hope so."

My partner walked with me to the ambulance. "Care to explain what that was all about?" He asked.

"Well she has a nosebleed for two hours and everyone's thinking she's going to have to go to the hospital to have her nose cauterized. Then we show up and a few minutes later the bleeding stops. I guess they thought one of us had something to do with it."

"Why would they think we had anything to do with it?"

"There's a story in the Bible, I believe it's in Acts, Chapter 5, where sick people were brought out into the streets because people believed that if the shadow of Peter fell across them, they would be healed. Apparently, they knew the sick could be healed by the mere presence of someone who carried God's power walking past them."

"And they think one of us has that kind of power?"

"Yes they do. Pretty crazy, huh?"

As we drove back to town I wondered if that was what we had just seen. The firefighters were convinced that it was, but I wasn't completely sold on the idea yet. In spite of my doubts, I thanked God for His great mercy and healing power.

Burning Pinkies

AFTER SPENDING YEARS IN A church where the presence of God was absent, we started attending a church where we began to feel and see unusual things. It didn't take long before we realized we were feeling the tangible presence of God. My wife and I began to ask The Holy Spirit to bring His presence into our living room and sure enough, we could feel His presence show up every time we asked. This was a radical thing to us.

Although I'd been an atheist until I was 38 years old, after I became a believer I loved to debate with people about the reality of God's existence. I once talked for 12 hours straight about God with an EMT that I worked with. We covered the subject from every angle I could think of. She was happy to talk and listen, but at the end of the day she was no more convinced about the existence of God. The apostle Paul said his message did not come in excellence of speech, but also in the demonstration of God's power. (1 Cor. 2:4)

It was the power of God that was missing from my argument. Words are necessary to convey ideas, but the argument needs some kind of evidence. Christians talk about a personal God who interacts with them, but when we tell our friends about God, we often have no personal experience (evidence) for them. God needs to show up and do something.

My wife and I began going to her hair styling appointments together. She likes having me along partly because she knows I'll have a few fun stories to tell her stylist, Angie, who is open to discussions about God and the supernatural. While she did my wife's hair, we talked about miracles and even about some resurrection stories we had heard.

I figured it was safe to talk about resurrection because Angie used to work for a funeral home and worked around dead bodies. The discussion was going well, so I told her we would show her evidence of God's existence before we left.

I knew Angie suffered from chronic neck pain, because we'd talked about it before. I thought maybe God would heal her neck that night. When it was time, I told her we would ask God to bring His presence into the room so she could know He was real and experience Him personally. I wanted to prepare her for the experience, but I didn't want to coach her into feeling something that wasn't God. I explained that we did this before with others and described what they felt. I described what His presence feels like to me, and my wife shared what it feels like to her. We told her it's a little different for everyone.

We all stood with our hands out and our eyes closed. I began: "Holy Spirit, bring your presence." I waited about 30 seconds to let her sense His presence then continued, "Holy Spirit, bring your power to heal." We waited a few minutes then opened our eyes and talked about what we felt.

"Wow. That was so weird." Angie said. "As soon as you asked God's presence to come, I felt something like a force pushing me forward. I was thinking to myself, 'I'm gonna fall over,' and I was telling the force, 'hey, knock it off'."

"That's the presence of God that you're feeling. I can feel it too. It makes me sway back and forth. Do you feel anything else right now?"

"Yeah. I feel a burning sensation in both of my pinkie fingers. It's not uncomfortable; it's just really warm. It started in my fingers and traveled down the outside of my hands and into my wrists." She placed her fingers on her cheeks to see if the heat was real.

I thought for a moment then asked, "Do you have carpal tunnel syndrome?"

Her eyes grew bigger. "Yeah, how did you know? I'm ambidextrous, so I have it in both wrists." God was healing her carpal tunnel as we talked about it (not her neck pain, as I thought He would.)

∽

My wife continued seeing Angie for several more years and her wrists remained healed.

I've Fallen and I Can't Get Up

As I drove to work I wondered who would be healed today. God had been doing more miracles through me when I asked people if they wanted prayer. Healing wasn't just an occasional thing anymore, but a lifestyle. We checked out the ambulance and made sure all our equipment was working then called dispatch to let them know we were ready for our first call. I wondered if it would be someone with a foot injury or maybe back pain.

Our first call was for a woman who fell while attempting to cross the busiest street in town. She didn't make it very far. We found her laying half on the curb and half in the street in the pouring rain. We quickly put her on a backboard and got her in the ambulance where it was dry. I got her medical history and asked what happened.

"Well, I was walking down the sidewalk with my cane. I use it because I have trouble feeling the irregularities in the sidewalk. I have neuropathy in my right foot. I guess I didn't notice a big bump, and I tripped over it. I have an appointment to see a specialist tomorrow. He's going to do a procedure on my foot and I'll be using a walker after that."

"Would you mind if I prayed for your foot to be healed? Maybe you won't need surgery."

She smiled. "Get over here and take my hands. Let's get this done!"

I placed my hand on her foot. "Spirits of pain I command you to leave. Nerves come back to life, in the name of Jesus. Do you feel anything different?"

"My foot doesn't feel as swollen as it was a few minutes ago."

"Swelling, I command you to leave. Nerves, be healed in Jesus' name.

Okay, how does it feel now?"

She reached down to recheck the swelling. "I think all the swelling is gone, but it still feels numb."

I place my hand on her foot again. "Numbness I command you to leave in the name of Jesus. Nerves, be healed right now! Any changes yet?"

"There's like this wave of... I don't know... electricity going down my leg. The feeling is coming back."

I looked in her eyes. "In case you didn't know it, God really loves you." I didn't need to tell her. With tears of joy streaming down her cheeks, she softly said, "I know He does."

Who will be healed today? The choice is ours. If we don't lay hands on people in prayer, the answer is "nobody."

Meet Me at the Cemetery

WE CAME TO THE SPIRITUAL Hunger Conference expecting to see some cool things. We hoped to receive instruction and an impartation. Bill Johnson, the keynote speaker, gave a message on the kingdom of God each of the first three days. Bill's mannerisms make him one of a kind. With a warm smile and wavy salt and pepper hair, he delivers short, pithy sentences that make a deep impact on those who "get" him. When he delivers one of these zingers, he always waits a moment for it to sink in before moving on. During the opening night's message, he mentioned the kingdom of God at least 20 times, but never mentioned the *church* once. There is a difference. Jesus was a passionate teacher on the kingdom of God but only rarely did He mention the church. That's something I had to spend a little time thinking about.

We left the hotel room early each morning and came back late every night, tired, but spiritually stronger. I had brought along a few books and my guitar. It's not really a vacation unless you return home with clothes you didn't wear and books you didn't read.

It seemed like everywhere we went we made friends. During the intermissions we'd grab a cup of coffee and sit outside on the grass in front of the conference center. Before long seven or eight people would be sitting with us and we'd be talking excitedly about what was going on. During each session we saw blind and deaf people healed and crippled people get up out of wheelchairs. Before each speaker gave their message we'd spend a half hour worshipping our hearts out. I was surprised at one thing God did to me during worship. I saw many people laughing, jumping and being uninhibited during the conference. I was a little jealous. So God came after me during worship. The spirit of laughter came over me repeatedly and I went into fits of uncontrollable laughing. The joy I experienced during worship was greater than any joy I'd ever known.

I had a dramatic increase in visions while I was at the conference. For several years I'd been able to see things in the spirit when I closed my eyes, but at the conference my spiritual eyesight went into overdrive. I saw waves of power sweeping over the crowd during worship as well as a mist or fog settling over the crowd during a message. I saw a lot of heavenly scenes and demonic images. I became much more aware of the nature of the spiritual battle we are in.

We were involved in the "Treasure Hunt" workshop one afternoon. Having done them before, we were asked to lead a group who hadn't. We spent a few minutes asking God for clues, and then we set out looking for people to bless based on the clues we received from God. I had a couple of visions: In one I saw a bend in a river with geese swimming on it, and in the other vision I saw two people, one with red hair and one with black hair. The river was right behind the conference center. One of the guys in our group had an impression of flowers. There were hanging flower baskets on the bridge over the river that led to a park. We took off across the bridge and found two women sitting in the grass on the other side of the bridge, one with red hair, and one with black, like I saw in the vision. We prayed with them for healing.

One of the men in our group had some very specific clues. He saw the Washington monument, an alligator purse and the word "patient." We left the convention center and headed west, not really knowing which way we should be going. Downtown Spokane is brimming with shops and businesses. My eyes scanned the signs above each entrance hoping to see some business connected to the word "patient." We had only walked a block when we came to Washington Street. From there we could see an optometrist office two blocks away and felt that was where the patient might be. There was actually a sign above the door we entered that said, "Patient Entrance." There were two women in the waiting room—both had alligator purses. The first woman didn't want prayer, but the second one suffered migraines. After we explained what we were doing she let us pray with her.

We continued the hunt at a café. We weren't picking up any more leads so we decided to give our waitress some encouraging prophetic words that she gladly received.

We witnessed about 200 people healed each night at the conference. It was hosted by the International Association of Healing Rooms in Spokane, Washington. Their facility is located on the original site of the healing rooms built by John G. Lake, who was one of the most prolific healers who ever lived. The healing rooms he founded in the early 1900s saw over 100,000 people healed during a span of five years. Lake's gravesite is located in Spokane. During worship on the second day of the conference I heard the Lord tell me to go visit Lake's grave. He said He'd meet me there. At the conference, we connected with a group of new friends: Robert, his son Jeramy, and a woman named Gwendolyn. The five of us drove to the cemetery to find Lake's gravesite. Once we arrived, we spent a few moments in silence seeking God's presence.

The spirit of prophecy descended upon the group. We spent the next three hours prophesying to everyone who came near us. You wouldn't think there would be a lot of traffic at a cemetery in Spokane, but people drove up one after another and parked, saying that God told them He'd meet them at Lake's gravesite. The company of prophetic people grew to about ten or twelve. As people left, a few more would arrive. We formed a circle and put one person after another in the middle, giving them the words we heard from God.

As we put my wife in the center of the circle, people began to give her the impressions they received from the Lord. I saw an image of a beautiful lighthouse. "Honey, the Lord says you are a bright, shining beacon of light to everyone who comes near you."

As I was speaking a man drove up and rolled down his window. "Hey, I just wanted to share something with you all. As I was driving by I saw this brilliant column of white light coming from the center of your circle. I don't know what you're doing, but you should probably keep doing it." He rolled up his window and drove away.

The five of us remained together for the rest of the conference. We went to lunch and dinner together and prophesied to the waitresses who served us. Between speakers we sat on the lawn outside and prophesied to friends and strangers. We couldn't help but notice that being in an atmosphere of healing and the prophetic brought us into a new and deeper place with God.

Weather Report

SO MANY THINGS HAPPENED DURING the Spiritual Hunger Conference in Spokane. It really was a time of learning and growth for my wife and me. God had us doing things we had never considered before.

Prior to driving across Washington State to the conference, I had received an e-mail from my brother who lives in Nashville, Tennessee. There had been severe flooding in the Southeast. Atlanta had received 21 inches of rainfall in just a couple of days. My brother suggested that I should ask God to stop the rain. As I left the hotel Friday morning for the conference, I walked through the lobby and heard the weather forecaster talking on television about the flooding in the Southeast. Then I heard a still, small voice say, "Why don't you do something about it?"

I was a little shocked at hearing this from what I knew was the voice of the Holy Spirit. I had a quiet conversation with Him: "What do you mean 'why don't I do something about it?' I'm not God, *you* are. Why don't *you* do something about it?"

As I walked through the lobby Saturday morning I heard the weather forecaster talk about the continued flooding and again I heard God say, "Why don't you do something about it?"

Once more I quietly replied to Him, "How am I supposed to stop a storm thousands of miles away? Lord, if you want that storm to stop, why don't *you* do something about it?"

I didn't really believe in this kind of thing at the time, but I asked Robert, Jeramy, and Gwendolyn about it. Robert shared one of his experiences. "One time we were going to the coast and the forecast was for cloudy weather with highs in the 50s. I didn't want that. I wanted sunny weather with highs in the 60s so I made some declarations to that effect and when we got to the coast, it was sunny and stayed sunny the entire time we were there." Gwendolyn added a few of her own stories about commanding the weather to change and reminded me about the time Jesus calmed the storm on the Sea of Galilee. It was her view that we had authority to do anything He did. Bill Johnson said something Friday that gave me more confidence: "When you're hearing God's voice and you declare what you hear from heaven, you become the voice of God. All creation obeys you."

We decided to go for it.

Saturday morning we stood on the conference center lawn and put our plan into action. Directing my voice to the sky I spoke: "I command the storm in the Southeast United States to move, in Jesus' name. I command the winds of change to move the low-pressure system out to sea over the Atlantic Ocean, in Jesus' name. Atmosphere, obey the voice of the children of God!" The others stood beside me on the lawn making similar declarations.

I'm sure we looked more than a little nutty making decrees and declarations for a storm to cease while standing under the clear blue skies over Spokane, but I didn't care. I was coming to the realization that it didn't matter what strangers thought of me. I needed to do what I felt God asked me to do.

Excited to see if our declarations and commands were fruitful, we gathered around the television Sunday morning in the lobby of the hotel to check the weather. As the radar loop played, we could plainly see the storm front that had been stalled for weeks over the Southeast was now moving out to sea. Sunday's forecast was for plenty of sunshine.

We went to the conference expecting to receive from others. Although we were young in the prophetic life, God used us often to bless others and that surprised us. We saw ourselves as newbies who required more training and mentoring before we would be able to be used in ministry. Apparently God didn't see it that way. It was amazing to see the hand of God moving in power as we stepped out and followed His lead. We'll always be growing and learning. We'll always have need of spiritual fathers and mothers. But God can use us (and you) every step of the way while we're growing.

A Change of Heart

FOR MANY YEARS, MY BODY showed signs of a medical condition that I recognized as paroxysmal supraventricular tachycardia (PSVT.) In this condition, the heart has an extra pathway that allows electrical impulses to flow through it at a very fast rate. During episodes of PSVT, the heart rate can rise to over 200 beats per minute. Another characteristic is that it comes on for no apparent reason. I knew the condition was treatable with medication to control the heart rate or by having an "ablation" procedure performed, which destroys the pathway that causes the increased heart rate. I never wanted to be officially diagnosed and never spoke to my own doctor about it, but I had discussed treatment options with a cardiologist I met in my travels to and from hospitals on the job.

There was reluctance on my part to receive treatment; I preferred to manage it myself. When I was younger, I could make an episode go away by coughing or holding my breath. As I grew older these measures were of no help. For many years, I just remained in limbo about this health issue, not wanting to see a doctor because I had seen the side effects some patients suffer with medication or ablation. Later in my life, when I became convinced that God wanted to heal us of our medical problems I began to ask Him to heal my heart.

As I mentioned in the previous stories, I attended a spiritual conference in Spokane on the last weekend of September 2009. My wife and I went there hoping to be healed of some chronic neck and back pain. On Friday the 25th, I went forward to the stage area during worship; it was a powerful experience. When I closed my eyes I saw a vision of a credit card and silver and gold coins. Based on my history of visions and dreams from God, I believed He was asking me to give a large donation that night. I asked about a specific amount to give but God didn't give me a number. After worship, I made my way back to my seat. I began to discuss the donation amount with my wife and she got out our checkbook.

"How much should we donate?"

"How much did we give last night?" I asked. She leaned over and whispered the amount in my ear.

"Well maybe we should give ten times that much."

My wife is usually the one who is prompted by God with an amount to give. We discussed it briefly and she began writing the date and payee on the check. Before she filled in the amount, I went into an episode of PSVT. My heart quickly hit a racing speed and I broke out in a sweat. I tried coughing and holding my breath but it wasn't working, so I told my wife what was happening. She took one look at me, promptly dropped the checkbook, and began to lay hands on me in prayer. Friends and people sitting near us quickly joined in.

The pounding in my chest felt like someone was hitting me with a hammer, making it hard to breathe. A volunteer noticed what was going on and asked if I wanted them to call for an ambulance. I sensed God wanted to do something and the last thing I needed was a visit to the emergency department. I said, "No, don't call. I'm a paramedic." About 20 minutes went by and nothing had changed. I began to hear God speak to me again about making a large donation. I sensed my healing was hovering over me and it would come when I took a step of faith.

I turned to my wife and said, "Stop praying for me and fill out the check."

She seemed stunned that I would want her to stop praying and really didn't like the idea of putting the donation ahead of my healing. Turning to the woman sitting next to her, she asked her to pray for me in her place. Because I seemed so intent about it, she grabbed the checkbook off the floor and filled in our offering amount. I was watching her write the numbers and as soon as she filled in the dollar amount, the episode of PSVT ended. We all breathed a sigh of relief and gave a shout of praise to God. As I sat there, I began to have a feeling that I was healed permanently of my condition.

As I tried to focus on the next speaker on the platform, I noticed that my pulse was irregular. It wasn't fast; it was just very irregular, like it is when I've checked the pulse on a patient in atrial fibrillation. I've never had an irregular pulse, not even an occasional skipped beat. Although I was feeling happy and comfortable, my pulse remained oddly irregular the rest of the night. As I pondered what might be causing it, a few questions for God came to the surface. I told Him I never had an irregular pulse before and wanted to know what was going on. His reply sounded something like this; "Are you telling me your old heart never had an irregular heartbeat? Maybe your heartbeat is different now because you have a new heart." This filled me with joy and wonder for the rest of the evening. I began to believe in my healing, hoping it was permanent. When I went to bed after midnight, I checked my pulse and it was still irregular. When I awoke in the morning my pulse was normal again. I believe the irregularity of my pulse for several hours was a sign to let me know something in my heart had been permanently changed.

I shouldn't have been surprised that God healed my heart, but I really was astounded. Another surprise was waiting for me when I got home from the conference. I received an unexpected refund check from the state. It was for twice the amount we gave the night I was healed.

Jesus defeated Satan in the wilderness. He took his private victory and shared with all who would receive it. It's a spiritual principle that applies to us. Having been given victory over this problem, I can now share my story with other patients who need faith and hope for their own heart difficulties. This week I prayed with a man who was going to have a quadruple bypass. We asked God to give him a new heart so he could avoid surgery.

I'd like to state that I don't believe we can "buy" our healing from God. No amount of money or good works can secure divine healing; it's an act of grace. Jesus already paid the price for us to be healed. All we can do is ask and receive it. I didn't know what the end result would be. I came to the conference for other health problems but God knows which ones take priority and I'm happy to yield to His greater knowledge. Having said that, I also know that God rewards faithfulness and obedience, sometimes in unexpected ways.

Casey's Story

PRIOR TO 2008, NEARLY EVERY paramedic, firefighter, and emergency room nurse in two counties knew Casey on a first name basis. His alcoholic antics were the stuff of legends. It was common for him to be transported to a hospital three or four times a day. Ambulances were routinely dispatched for "Casey sightings." Some crews would transport him without being dispatched to get him into the emergency department early in the shift so they wouldn't have to pick him up at three in the morning.

EMT and Paramedic instructors took special time in their classes to teach students how to properly transport Casey. According to the state, his healthcare bill at the expense of taxpayers exceeded ten million dollars by the mid 1990s.

In an effort to reign in the expense of treating homeless alcoholics in Tacoma, Washington, the two largest hospitals developed a jointly funded project called the "Sobering Center." Staffed by one employee, it has five rooms designated as safe places for drunks to be transported instead of sending them to a hospital. The rooms have a mattress on the floor and bathroom facilities. Guests are watched for several hours then released to the community. This project was developed largely to address the problems caused by Casey's drinking. If ever an alcoholic had earned status as a legend, it was Casey.

While transporting him from a hospital to detox a few years ago, I had a "God encounter" with him. I asked God to give me some words that would forever change his life. I felt that God's sullied reputation in Tacoma could somehow be redeemed if He could get Casey to quit drinking. During the transport, God gave me a few things to say to him. When we arrived at detox, I got out of the driver's seat and climbed in back. I sat on the bench seat next to him.

"Casey... I have a message for you from God. Do you want to hear it?"

Dressed in clean clothes for the first time in months and completely sober he replied, "Sure."

"People have been calling you a worthless drunk all your life and you've always believed it. Well I'm here to tell you that every word spoken about you being a useless drunk is a lie. You need to stop listening to those lies. They're from the pit of hell. God didn't make you a useless drunk, Casey. He made you to be a sober man of integrity that other people would respect. God made you to be a pillar of society. One day you're going to walk into a treatment center and your testimony is going to set other people free of alcoholism. People are going to look to you as an example of how to get free of alcohol." I prophesied non-stop for about ten minutes that he would have a new future.

He sat in stunned silence as I spoke and when I was finished he said, "Thanks."

A little more than six months later, in March of 2009 I saw Casey in the emergency department. He was there for a minor injury. And he was sober. Now it was *my* turn to be stunned. I went to the desk and asked the nurses about it. Four different nurses confirmed that he'd been clean and sober for almost six months.

Four months later I was talking with a Tacoma cop at one of the hospitals. I mentioned that I'd heard Casey was clean and sober. He said, "Yup, that's a fact. We see him every day at 11:45 walking down Ninth Street to the Urban Grace Church to his AA meetings. He looks like a different man."

For over a year, I hoped to find Casey and ask what happened to him. In October of 2010, I spent one day following up on a few patients I had prayed with. While driving down Tacoma Avenue, I spotted Casey. I parked my car, got out and talked with him for about 30 minutes. He gave me permission to write his story. I changed his name to protect his privacy.

This is his story:

One night Casey was on the ground nearly dying while pounding on the door of the sobering center. He was desperately trying to be let in before they opened. After crashing from being drunk, he began vomiting blood. He thought it would stop, but the blood kept coming.

He tried to get the attention of the caretaker by pounding on the door, but she ignored him.

Filled with fear, he begged her again to open the door. When she did, she saw blood everywhere and called for an ambulance. The ambulance took him to the closest hospital. He was rushed to the operating room where they repaired his ruptured esophagus. After coming out of the hospital it was time for his wake-up call.

He thought about quitting his love affair with alcohol many times. After 23 failed attempts to get sober, he entered a treatment program. He was allowed to live in an apartment above detox. One day he went to Tim's convenience store to get beer. They wouldn't sell it to him so he cursed them out and left. He went across the street and bought a six-pack but as he came out of the store, the police saw him and took it away. He cursed them out. He looked around for his drinking friends but found none, so he hopped a bus to the south end of town and tried to buy beer at 38th street, but they wouldn't sell to him either. He cursed them out and left, a bitter man.

Lonely, empty, and sober, he caught the bus back to Fawcett Street. He had a stash of two bottles hidden in the bushes. He pulled them out and with determination in his mind never to drink again he dumped them on the ground. He went back to his apartment and fell asleep. Casey remained in treatment, went to his group meetings and hasn't had a drink in five years. His life of addiction was finally over.

He has bus passes to get around town but he doesn't use them much. While driving through town I see him hobbling down the sidewalk with his walker from time to time. He loves to walk. He can be seen every day going to the Urban Grace Church where his AA group meets. He even has a car that he paid cash for, but he doesn't use it much. He prefers to walk. Casey knows he's become a role model. He won't tell alcoholics, "Just do what I did." He believes we're all different and what worked for him, may not work for them. But he knows he was one of the worst alcoholics ever and he knows that if he was able to do it, anyone can.

I don't know if he has an intimate relationship with God at this point in his journey. When I last saw him several years ago he was still sorting things out, which is not surprising considering the life of abuse, addiction, and confusion he came from. Some changes take more time than others. Life's a journey. We can only take one step at a time.

Broken Shoulders & Broken Hearts

I TRANSPORT MANY PATIENTS FROM small hospitals to larger ones for special procedures. One of the most common procedures is a coronary angiogram for patients having chest pain. The place where this procedure is done is called a cath lab.

Despite the fact that she was wearing a hospital gown, our patient managed to keep her appearance tasteful. She had on fresh eye shadow and lipstick and her ebony hair was neatly combed. As we loaded her on the gurney I noticed a gold cross dangling from a chain around her neck. "That's a beautiful cross you're wearing."

"Oh thank you. I wear it as a reminder of God's faithfulness to me during the hard times I've been through."

"I know exactly what you mean," I replied. "I've been through years of difficult times myself and He's been so faithful to me."

"I don't know what I'd do if I didn't have Him," she said. "I'm so blessed to have a family who is lifting me up in prayer right now."

"Well, then you won't mind if I pray for you," I said.

"Oh, I would just love that."

I placed my hand on her left shoulder. She said, "Oh, do you want to start with my bad shoulder?"

I began laughing. "I'm sorry. I didn't know you had a shoulder problem. By any chance do you have a torn rotator cuff?"

"No, I have bursitis. My shoulder hurts all the time."

I gently placed my hand on her shoulder again. "I command bursitis to leave right now in the name of Jesus. Spirit of pain, get out now." I asked if she felt any changes.

"Well, it feels wonderful! It doesn't hurt at all."

"Isn't God just awesome?"

"He's been so good to me," She replied with a smile.

Since she had just been healed of bursitis, I wanted to go for something a little bigger. She had been admitted to the hospital for breathing problems related to heart failure. She's lived with diabetes for many years. I wanted to see if we could get everything healed.

"You know, since God already healed your shoulder, I was thinking maybe we should try to get the rest of you healed. Can I pray for your heart to be healed?"

"I would love that."

I placed my hand on her newly healed shoulder. "Holy Spirit I ask you to bring your power upon this woman and I bless your work of healing in her body. Heart be healed. Pancreas and liver be healed. Lungs be healed in the name of Jesus." I asked again if she felt any different.

"I feel at peace," She replied.

"That's the Prince of Peace letting you know that He's working on your healing. I should probably tell you about something before we get to the hospital. Once you're healed, the symptoms may return. If you notice you're healed one day and the symptoms come back, don't be worried that you were not healed. Your healing is real, but healing is a battle and sometimes spirits of pain and sickness will try to make you think you weren't healed. Refuse to receive the symptoms again and tell those demons to leave. You may have to do it more than once." She seemed to understand.

"By the way, this is something any believer can do. You saw how I commanded pain to leave, right? Well you can get people healed the same way I did. It's so easy anyone can do it." She was excited to learn anything I could share with her.

We arrived at the hospital and wheeled her inside. She gave me a warm hug before she got off the gurney and I introduced her to the cath lab team.

A Sticky Subject

ONE SEPTEMBER NIGHT I WENT with my wife to the hair salon. As Angie did my wife's hair, her son sat on a chair playing a video game while I shared some of the things God had been doing with us. We had been seeing people healed in grocery stores and restaurants and Angie was always interested in hearing the latest God stories.

I took advantage of a pause in our conversation to watch Angie's son, who was riveted to his video game. I wondered what he thought about miracles and about God.

"Hey Angie, do you have a penny?" I asked.

"A penny? For what?"

"I want to show your son something."

My wife glanced at me and smiled. She knew exactly what I was going to do. Angie opened her cash box and gave me a penny. I found a place on the wall, and held the penny in place two or three times and watched it fall to the floor. We had learned how the manifest presence of God allows coins to stick to the wall at a friend's house a few weeks earlier, but I had forgotten one thing: invite the Holy Spirit to join us.

"Lord, bring your presence into this room and make yourself known to us."

I held the penny to the wall and it stuck, for about five seconds. Angie's mouth hung open in shock.

"Hey... how did you do that?"

I picked the penny up off the floor and placed it on the wall again, asked the Holy Spirit to hold it there and it stuck again. Her son looked up and smiled. I did it a third time. "Holy Spirit, take this penny and hold it to the wall when I let go of it." Once again it stuck to the wall for about five seconds.

"Is this some kind of trick?" Angie asked.

I moved over to the corner of the wall and let half the penny hang over the edge. "Holy Spirit, take this penny." It stuck for about one second. I picked it up, repeated it three or four times, and her son dropped his game and came over to stand beside me.

"How did you do that?" He asked.

"Jesus said that signs and wonders would follow those who believe in Him. I believe in Him and this is one of those signs. It's not magic; it's the power of God. You can do the same thing."

I demonstrated a few more times, and then he held it to the wall and asked God to hold it when he let go. It stuck the first time and every time afterward. He was so amazed he forgot about his video game.

People often ask, "What's the point of all this?"

I found out that night that there are several valuable things that come from these exercises. First, sticking pennies to the wall is a tangible display of God's power that's difficult to refute by natural explanations. It's a great introduction for those who don't know Him.

Second, it's an exercise in which we learn to cooperate with God and sense his presence and power at work. Angie's son knows virtually nothing about the power of God. But after last night, he has at least one way in which he can experience God. As curious as boys are, it won't be long before he finds other ways to relate to Him.

Third, as we cooperate with God, our faith for operating in miracles, signs, and wonders grows. If we start with a simple thing like this, it can grow in many different directions including things like food multiplication, healing, and raising the dead.

These exercises are like going to a gym and working out. Working out doesn't have a great purpose in itself. It's merely a way to strengthen yourself so you can operate better when you do other things. In the same way, sticking coins to the wall has no real purpose in itself, it's merely a way to exercise your spiritual muscles and grow in faith.

Sticking coins to the wall builds faith for living a kingdom lifestyle. If you spend an afternoon with friends getting to know God's power by sticking things to the wall, the next time you need to release God's power for a person with cancer, you might be surprised by how much faith you have for healing.

Healing My Partner

AFTER A FEW DAYS OFF work, I came back one day to find my EMT partner hobbling toward the ambulance at the start of our first call. He winced in pain as we lifted the gurney. "What's wrong with you?" I asked.

Rather than answer my question, he asked his own question. "Do you know if our company provides short-term disability benefits?"

"Why do you want to know?"

"I hurt my back on our last shift. My lower back is killing me and the pain goes down the back of my leg. I'm pretty sure I blew out a disc, so I need to know if my time off work is going to be compensated."

"If you have a job-related injury, and you need to take time off work for rehab, you'll be paid for it, but it will only be about half of what you're being paid now."

I could tell that my answer didn't give him much hope. After our first call, we made it back to our station, where he collapsed in a recliner. He had already been healed on four previous occasions while on duty: once from a headache, once from neck pain, another time from back pain and you read the story about his hand injury from a broken tree branch. I walked over to where he was sitting and went for healing number five.

"Where's the pain the worst?"

He pointed to his lower back. "Right here."

I had him lean forward and I placed my hand on the middle of his back. "I command the spirit of pain and the spirit of trauma to leave right now in the name of Jesus." As I walked away I added, "You're healed, now stop being a sissy."

Later that day (after we ran a few more calls) I asked how he felt. He reported that all the pain and muscle spasms were gone. I checked with him again a few days later and the pain never returned. My friend had many concerns: would he require surgery? How would the injury affect his life at home? Would he lose a few months of work while going through physical therapy or rehabilitation?

Forget all that worry and hassle. No doctor's appointment. No MRI. No pain medications or time off work. None of them came to pass, thanks to a God who heals.

Electric Blues

I HAVE A YOUNG FRIEND who was dating my stepson for a period of time. One winter day she drove her old Volvo to our house and when she went to leave, her car would not start. It had been raining for days, and the hood didn't close completely, so the engine compartment was soaking wet. I put a tarp over it and tried the best I could to dry it out, but the car still wouldn't start.

I decided to see if there was anything that needed to be repaired or replaced. The spark plugs looked okay, but the spark plug wires showed cracks in the wiring so I replaced them. I also replaced the distributor cap, but the rotor was stuck and couldn't be replaced, so I cleaned the electrical contacts to make sure it would carry a spark to the distributor cap. None of this seemed to help and even after a day without rain, the car still wouldn't start.

During this time my friend's faith in God was wavering. I did my best to cheer her up.

"Maybe God will work a car miracle for you and get it running again."

"We've prayed. I think if He was going to, He would have done it already," she replied crossly. She was very stressed out over the situation because she didn't have a lot of money to have the car repaired. We invited her to stay at our house until we could get it running again, but after three days we were all beginning to lose our sanity over this car problem. We all had been fussing over the car, praying and trying to start it.

In a moment of total frustration my stepson went out to her car, got in and closed the door. He said, "Okay God, do you see your daughter's desperation? I'm already angry about this and we've done everything we can!" Slamming his fist on the dashboard, he said, "In the name of Jesus, I command this car to start!" He then put the keys in the ignition and gave them a turn. VROOM! The car started right up.

Not long after this, his girlfriend had been helping him unload some electronic equipment he bought. While carrying an oscillator into the house, she dropped it on the floor and it broke. He tested it but every time he turned it on, it tripped the breaker. This meant it was shorted out. We gathered around it and everyone prayed over it in the hope it would be fixed.

"Father, we know you want to bless your children and we know you healed the Volvo. We ask for the help of angels to fix this broken oscillator. We command the wiring and circuits to be repaired, so we would have a testimony to your goodness."

My stepson plugged it in, but it tripped the breaker again. We prayed again, but again it tripped the breaker when he plugged it in. We put it aside and went about our lives. A couple of hours later my stepson's girlfriend decided to pray over it one more time. She prayed and asked him to plug it in and it didn't trip the breaker. He ran a few tests on it and it was working normally.

God sees our situation and His heart is to help us, no matter what needs to be fixed. Whether it's raising the dead or fixing a car, He wants to meet all our needs.

Attention Walmart Shoppers

MY WIFE AND I TOOK a trip to eastern Washington to celebrate our anniversary. Late September is the perfect time to visit the Cascade Mountains, as the vine and broadleaf maples are usually at their peak of fall color. On the first morning of our vacation, we stopped at Walmart to pick up a power cord for my cell phone. To no one's surprise, we found someone who needed healing.

Walmart seems to be a sanctuary for people with physical problems. You can always find someone wearing an immobilizer or cast, walking with a cane, or in a wheelchair. I have to confess; I've started looking for people with disabilities everywhere I go and Walmart is a great place to find people who need healing. This morning we found an elderly couple hobbling through the store in obvious pain. The gentleman was using a cane and his wife was leaning on a shopping cart for support.

I love my wife's patience with me. Like a toddler with a new toy, I asked her if we could take time to pray for them. She said yes despite the fact that this might delay our plans for the day. There's a little bit of anxiety you must deal with when you walk up to strangers and ask if they want to be healed. Vincent Van Gogh once said, *"If you hear a voice within you say 'you cannot paint' then by all means paint and that voice will be silenced."* There's a similar voice inside of us saying, "You cannot heal strangers." I've learned to heal strangers in spite of that voice and over time it has been silenced.

"Good morning, how are you folks doing today?"

The woman replied, "We're doing okay I guess. Isn't the weather just beautiful this morning?"

"It's a glorious day. The fall colors are amazing. Say, I noticed you both seem to have some health problems. My wife and I pray for a lot of people in stores and we see quite a few of them healed."

"You mean you pray for people right in the store? I've never heard of that. What church do you go to?"

"We're from out of town. We came here to celebrate our wedding anniversary." Turning to her husband I asked, "Sir, may I ask how you injured yourself?"

"Years ago I had a little accident with a logging truck. It's a long story but it did a lot of nerve damage and left me partly paralyzed."

"How about you, ma'am?"

"I have neuropathy in my feet from diabetes. I've also had a couple of bouts with cancer but God got me through them. He's been so good to me."

"Sir, do you mind if I pray with you to be healed?"

"That would be alright with me."

"Are you having any pain right now?"

"I sure am. My back hurts all the time." Smiling and pointing at his wife he continued, "That's why I'm using her cane to walk."

"On a scale from one to ten with ten being the worst pain you can imagine, how bad is your pain right now?"

"Oh, I'd say maybe a five or six."

My wife and I placed our hands on his back. Curious shoppers walked by. A few shook their heads or rolled their eyes at us. I tried not to let their reactions bother me. "I command pain to leave right now in the name of Jesus. Nerves, tendons, ligaments and muscles be healed right now. Holy Spirit I bless your work of healing in this man. Lord, bring your presence upon him. Spirits of pain I command you to leave." After a few minutes of prayer I asked how he felt. He shifted his weight from side to side and walked in a small circle in front of us. Slowly, a smile began to appear on his weathered face.

"Well that's the darndest thing. I don't seem to be hurting at all."

I couldn't contain my joy and yelled out, "Yay, Jesus!" I began laughing and turned to his wife. "How about you ma'am? Are you ready to be healed?"

"Why not?" She replied with a smile.

We prayed for his wife and within a few minutes she also felt nearly complete relief of her symptoms. As we were about to let them finish their shopping, they wanted our names and e-mail address, so we exchanged information, prayed a blessing over their finances and relationships and went our separate ways.

We found a power cord for my cell phone, but I wouldn't have cared if we didn't find one. I left the store overjoyed that I have a friend like Jesus who heals people. His power is more than enough for me.

New Wine

MY WIFE AND I SPENT a romantic weekend in the town of Leavenworth, Washington, to celebrate our anniversary. Leavenworth is a Bavarian theme town nestled on the eastern slopes of the Cascade Mountains. The downtown area is a bustling shopping district that draws tourists from around the world. Hanging baskets of petunias, fuchsias and geraniums adorn the street corners. Eastern Washington is famous for its apple orchards and in recent years it's earned a reputation for its wines. One morning while strolling through the shops in the downtown area, we spotted a quaint little store that sold locally bottled wines. A sign in the window invited visitors in to sample their newest vintage, so we went inside.

We struck up a conversation with the woman behind the counter who poured the wine samples.

"What are you folks in town for?"

"We're celebrating our anniversary by healing people with injuries."

"Well that's different. Can I interest you in a sample of one of our wines?"

"Sure. Do you have anything on the sweet side?"

"We have a nice Riesling that you might like." She got a glass and poured while I thought about asking her my next question.

"You don't happen to have any chronic pain do you?"

"No... well, except for my shoulder. I can't raise my right arm up very high without it hurting on top of my shoulder."

"Do me a favor? Raise your right arm as high as you can without causing it to hurt." She raised it almost exactly 90 degrees, straight out from her body. My wife and I recognized this as one of the classic signs of "frozen shoulder" also called adhesive capsulitis. Raising the arm up brings severe pain in the shoulder.

"I'll bet you have frozen shoulder. It may have begun with a rotator cuff injury. Have you had an MRI yet?"

"No. I just live with the pain. I'm afraid to find out what's wrong."

"You don't have to live with the pain. We've seen a lot of people healed of the same injury you have. In fact, my wife had frozen shoulder once. For her it all started with a torn rotator cuff."

My wife explained that after her diagnosis, she rejected the surgery for the torn muscle. She said, "Instead, we went to visit a couple from our church and I was healed after about 30 minutes of prayer!"

I jumped in and asked the woman, "Do you mind if I pray for you? It won't take 30 minutes."

"I don't mind at all."

I like to close my eyes briefly to see if the Holy Spirit will show me a vision about what's going on with the person or their injury. In this instance, I didn't see anything "in the spirit" so I opened my eyes and commanded pain and inflammation to leave. I commanded healing of the tendons, muscles, ligaments and cartilage. It went very quickly. I asked if she felt anything.

"What do you mean?"

"Do you feel any heat or tingling in your shoulder?"

With a little hesitation she answered, "Not really."

"I'd like you to do something. Would you try to raise your arm up as high as you can?" (I raised mine to show her how I wanted her to do it.) She raised her arm up until it extended straight above her head. Her mouth dropped open in surprise.

"Oh my gosh! It doesn't hurt."

We stayed for about 20 more minutes and shared a little with her about some of our experiences with God. We told her about the elderly couple that had been healed at Walmart the previous day. We talked about wine and bought two bottles to take home with us. I bought the Riesling and my wife selected a bottle of Cabernet Sauvignon. This was just one of the many people we saw healed on our weekend getaway. Jesus made our vacation better than we expected.

Prophetic Hot Tub

THE SECOND DAY OF OUR anniversary vacation we got up early in the morning to have a soak in the hotel's hot tub, but we weren't alone. A mother was there with her four children. The two youngest children who were about ten years old were in the hot tub with us. It wasn't the most romantic setting, but I decided to make the best of it and wondered if God was up to something.

As I rested with my eyes closed, God gave me a vision about the boy. I saw him building things and using Tonka trucks. Then I saw large yellow construction equipment like backhoes and bulldozers. It seemed like God was telling me he likes to build things. I kept my eyes closed and asked God for some information about his sister and saw a scene that seemed to portray her future. I began a conversation with the boy about a safe subject to break the ice.

"Hey, did you have breakfast yet?"

"Yeah. It was really good!"

"What did you have?"

"Bacon!" He said with a huge smile, "and waffles."

"Bacon and waffles? Good choice. Hey, do you like to build things?"

He nodded his head.

"As I was sitting here resting, God gave me a vision about you. I think it's about your future."

His eyes grew bigger with anticipation.

Looking at his mother to see if she approved, I asked him, "Would you like to hear more?" His mom was all smiles.

He finally asked, "What did God tell you about me?"

"I think God is going to open doors for you in the construction business. Maybe it's something you're called to do—like a gift that you have. I think if you go into construction as a career, you'd probably find it rewarding and you'll probably be good at it." It was obvious no one had ever given him a prophetic word before.

His sister chimed in. "Did God show you anything about me?"

"As a matter of fact He did. He showed me a vision of you in the future. You looked like you were about 20 years old. I saw you dancing gracefully, like a ballerina. I think it's a special talent He's given you. If you choose to be a dancer I think God will make you successful at it." She was happy and very surprised to hear this coming from a stranger in a hot tub at a hotel.

Their mother, Jessie, was amazed at the fact that I knew these things about her kids.

"Where did you learn how to do this?"

"It's a long story, but a few years ago God began teaching me how to see visions from Him. Through visions He tells me secrets about people and I share what He shows me to give them hope, direction and comfort."

"Can you see visions for anyone or only certain people?"

"When I ask Him to show me something for a certain person He usually does. I pray for a lot of people to be healed and many times He shows me what's wrong with them through visions. I pray for their healing out of what He shows me."

Jessie's eyes lit up when I mentioned healing. "So do you see a lot of people healed?" We shared some of the stories about the healings we'd seen that weekend. "Wow, this is like a divine appointment or something. Do you think God would heal my vision?"

"I think He would. What's wrong with your vision?"

"I'm far-sighted and I hate wearing glasses."

My wife and I stepped out of the hot tub and moved to where Jessie was sitting. I placed my hand on her forehead above her eyes and commanded her vision to be restored. Next she asked me to pray for her older son who had symptoms of a cold. To be honest, I didn't expect a cold to be healed by prayer. But I prayed with the same faith I had all the other times this week.

I placed my hand gently on his head. "Cold virus I command you to leave now in the name of Jesus. Sinuses be healed. Inflammation leave. Spirits of sickness I command you to leave right now."

He looked at his mother and said that his nose, which was sore and runny a few minutes ago felt a lot better.

Before we left she had me give her oldest daughter a prophetic word. I saw her windsurfing off the coast of an island that looked like Hawaii (which turned out to be her favorite place.) In the vision I saw that she had confidence on her board and a look of determination on her face. She was moving very fast. Then I saw the front of a thin boat, like a kayak and a paddle going through the water. I gave her some insights from this vision and she was encouraged by it. Her mother said it described her very well.

Earnestly desire the best gifts, especially that you may prophesy... because you never know who will be blessed.

The Dr. Scholl's Anointing

WHEN WE'RE IN PAIN, MANY of us go to a hospital for treatment. But we all know someone who still has chronic pain even after being treated by a doctor. Given that healing is supposed to be our job as medical providers, I'm puzzled at how many nurses and doctors still live with chronic pain. On Labor Day weekend a few years ago, I met four different people who bring comfort to the sick while suffering from their own aches and pains.

On Friday, while picking up a patient at a hospital, I ran into a friend in the emergency department hallway. Kris is the kind of nurse that paramedics naturally like: a competent and skilled woman with a cheerful disposition and a wicked sense of humor. I've known her for years and I've always enjoyed her company. When she was diagnosed with cancer, I got to know her a little better.

She went through the usual regimen of chemo and radiation with a smile, which is not easy to do. Cancer treatment can be brutal. She's a survivor and a living testimony to the perseverance of the human soul. We were talking in the ER hallway, when she asked what I was up to. I shared some of the healing miracles I'd seen. She told me she had plantar fasciitis in both feet and lives with constant pain. She asked if I would pray for her feet to be healed.

I escorted her to a hallway out of the main traffic area near the x-ray department, so we wouldn't draw attention. I knelt down on the floor and placed my hands on her feet and quietly began to speak. "In the name of Jesus, I command these feet to be healed. Spirit of pain I command you to go. Inflammation leave right now, in Jesus' name!

Well that should do it. How do you feel?"

"Are you kidding me? My feet don't hurt at all. How did you do that?"

"I cheated. It was God... and He loves you very much."

I gave her some tips on how to keep her healing. "Look, here's the deal, Kris. The pain is gone right now but it may come back. If it returns, just do what I did to get you healed. Command the pain to leave in the name of Jesus." I had to see a patient, so she gave me a hug and we both went back to work.

The next day I was back at the same hospital. I asked a nurse if Kris was around. "She's not here today, she's on call. Can I leave a message for her?"

"I prayed for her to be healed yesterday. She was healed and I just wanted to see how she was feeling today."

"What was she healed of?"

"Uh, plantar fasciitis, why?"

"Will you pray for me, too? I have plantar fasciitis in both feet."

Now what do you suppose the odds are that I would find two nurses in a row with plantar fasciitis? I asked how bad the pain was and how long she'd had it, then knelt down on the floor and placed my hands on her feet. She said in a surprised tone, "Are you going to pray for me right now?"

"Do you want to be healed right now?"

"Well I guess so. I just thought maybe you'd go home and pray for me."

"Is there any reason why we can't get you healed now?" I didn't wait for a reply.

"I command these feet to be healed in Jesus' name. I command plantar fasciitis to leave. I command the spirit of pain to leave right now and don't come back. Inflammation get out now, in Jesus' name!"

She got out of her chair and began jumping up and down. "I can't believe it, I can't believe it! This is a miracle!"

"You just got healed by a Jewish carpenter who died 2000 years ago."

She was overwhelmed with gratitude. Tears of joy streamed down her face. We talked about God's love for her and I gave her a short lesson on how to keep her healing.

The next day I was back in the same emergency department picking up another patient. I was telling the charge nurse—who is also a long-time friend—about the miracles I'd seen at her hospital. She said, "You know, it's funny. I'm having pain in my foot right now. It started a few days ago." She'd been training for months to run a half marathon.

"Do you want me to pray for your foot?"

"I'd love it."

I took her foot in my hands and softly spoke. "I command this foot to be healed in Jesus' name. Pain and inflammation, I command you to leave."

"Thanks," she said as she gave me a hug. She had a lot to do and I had to see my patient so we went back to work. I don't know if she was healed.

The following day, I had a fourth opportunity. I was at a different hospital, talking with the staff while waiting for a patient I'd be transporting. Due to paperwork and other issues we often arrive before the patient is ready to go. I noticed that one of the nurses had big shoulders and biceps like I've seen with competitive swimmers, so I got her attention. "Hey, I have a stupid question for you. By any chance did you swim competitively in college?"

"No, but it's funny you asked; I was thinking about swimming today. I can't go to the gym anymore and I want to keep in shape."

"Why can't you go to the gym anymore?"

"Because I'm clumsy, I guess. I broke the fifth metatarsal in both my feet."

This had to be a setup. I softly repeated, "Broken metatarsal bones in both feet?"

She shot me an inquisitive grin. "Yeah, why?"

I got up and motioned for her to follow me. I walked down the hallway away from the nurse's desk. When we were far enough away, so that no one else could hear, I explained what happened earlier that weekend. "You can certainly pray for my feet," she said.

I tried to appear as if I was just looking at her feet. I'm not sure she was even paying attention as I whispered the commands for healing. After a few minutes I left and she went back to the nurse's station. I met my EMT partner by our patient's room and we loaded her on the gurney. He saw what I was up to. "Did she get healed?"

"I don't know. She didn't say anything."

As we were preparing to leave, she came over to us. "By the way, I wanted to thank you, my feet feel wonderful." She smiled and left.

I got into medicine in 1981 so I could help heal the sick and injured. Twenty-nine years later that dream finally came true. I'm not really a gifted person. I just decided to step out of my comfort zone and miracles met me there.

Charismatic Chiropractic

ON A DAY WHEN MY regular partner took a sick day, I worked with someone I didn't know. Cindy and I were having a slow day. We were five hours into the shift and hadn't run a call. We talked about a lot of different things, including one of my favorite subjects: dreams.

I shared one of the crazier dreams I'd had recently. "Hey Cindy, so I had this dream a while ago where I transported a man who had severe crushing injuries from a car accident. I loaded him in the ambulance and took him to a hospital, but I didn't do any kind of treatment for him. I didn't put him on a backboard or put a c-collar on him or start an IV. I just sat on the bench seat on the way to the hospital. When we got to the emergency department I took him into a treatment room and the doctor asked what I did for him on the way. I told him, 'I didn't do anything but I think he's healed.' The doctor went in and examined him then came back out and said there's nothing wrong with him. The funny thing was, I knew in the dream that the presence of God in the ambulance had healed all of his injuries. Crazy dream, huh?"

"That's pretty cool. Have you ever seen anyone healed like that?"

"Not like that, but I have prayed with people who have been healed. My regular partner was healed of neck and back pain and I prayed with two people in a row who were healed of plantar fasciitis."

"That's really interesting. I was in a car accident a few years ago; it was a rear-end collision. I was treated by a chiropractor and went through physical therapy, but nothing has really seemed to work. I still have pain all the time in my back between my shoulder blades."

"Would you like me to pray for you to be healed?"

"Yes I would."

I put my hand on the middle of her back. "Muscles, bones, nerves, tendons, discs and ligaments be healed now in the name of Jesus." I asked how she felt.

She shrugged her shoulders up and down a few times and twisted from side to side. "Wow, are you serious? It's all gone!"

"Really?"

"I'm not kidding. It feels great!"

We talked the rest of the shift about healing and what God was doing. I didn't preach at her or ask her to say the sinner's prayer. I didn't feel the Holy Spirit leading us in that direction. It was a low-key afternoon of conversations about everyday life. It just so happens that my everyday life is a little more supernatural than it once was. In getting her healed, I opened the door to the kingdom of God. It's her choice to decide if she's ready to go in. Perhaps she will. Maybe she won't. The Holy Spirit is more than able to guide her if she's ready.

Healing seems to be catching on and I'm encouraged by that. It shouldn't be about one person doing something unusual. Healing should be a normal thing that all believers are doing. It was normal for Jesus and His disciples and it should be normal for us. But if healing is going to return to being a normal Christian activity it's going to require more of us to leave the safety of the boat and walk out on the water. I hope you'll take a step of faith and heal someone in Jesus' name today.

∽

A few months later I ran into Cindy and asked how she felt. She was happy to report that the pain had not returned.

Praying for a Muslim

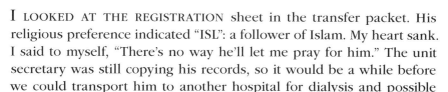

I LOOKED AT THE REGISTRATION sheet in the transfer packet. His religious preference indicated "ISL": a follower of Islam. My heart sank. I said to myself, "There's no way he'll let me pray for him." The unit secretary was still copying his records, so it would be a while before we could transport him to another hospital for dialysis and possible surgery. I went to his room to introduce myself.

Crammed into a room slightly larger than a closet, I found Maurice, a man in his thirties with some big medical problems. After passing large amounts of blood in his bowel movements for three days, he reluctantly came to the emergency department. He'd managed to flush most of his blood volume down the toilet.

A normal red blood cell count (RBC) is between 4.5 and 5.5. His was 1.6. His hemoglobin and hematocrit were critical. The doctor ordered a transfusion of six units of whole blood and called us to transport him to a larger hospital for surgery.

"Hi Maurice. How are you doing?"

"I've been better. Man, my head is killing me."

"Well that's not good. Hey look, we need to get you out of this room and onto our gurney and it's going to be a tight squeeze in this tiny room. If we got the gurney beside the bed do you think you could move over without help?"

"Yeah, no problem."

"Cool. And you need to be careful moving. We can't afford to lose that IV in your neck." An external jugular vein was the only IV access they could find.

"Hey Maurice, I need to ask you some questions. How long have you been on dialysis?"

"Since I was twenty-one. I was diagnosed with high blood pressure when I was fifteen. When I was eighteen I had my first stroke and spent two weeks in a coma. I was diagnosed with kidney failure when I was twenty-one and started dialysis a few months later."

"Are you serious? Dude, that's insane. I know guys twice your age who don't have any of those problems."

"Yeah, well my life has been pretty crazy so far."

Maurice was curious by nature. The moment we got in the ambulance the questions began. "Are the lights on?" He asked.

"Yes, but only on the left side because people don't appreciate bright lights in their eyes."

"Not the inside ones, I mean the ones on the outside. Are the red lights on?"

"Do you think we need them?"

"I don't know, what do you think?"

"We don't use red lights very often when we transport between hospitals. Most of our patients are pretty stable. Every time we turn those red lights on we increase our odds of getting in an accident. Some drivers see the red lights and they freak out. Some people actually drive off the road trying to get out of our way and end up hurting themselves. Look, you have some problems, but I don't think we need to use the lights and sirens this time."

"What's the difference between an EMT and a paramedic?" He asked.

"An EMT has about 100 hours of training. Usually they take a class that lasts three or four months. A paramedic has a lot more training. Most paramedic classes are a year in length with some extra classes like anatomy and general chemistry."

"What's the difference between a paramedic and a nurse?"

"Well, a nurse has a minimum of two years of education but some nurses go to college for four years. The training is different. Nurse training is aimed at hospital and nursing home care, while paramedic training specializes in treating people in their homes and in situations outside of a hospital or nursing home."

I really liked Maurice. He was a pleasant man in spite of his medical problems and he laughed at most of what I said. He didn't fit the stereotype of Muslims that I'd built in my mind. He was strangely... very much like me. In explaining the differences between paramedics, EMTs and nurses, I told him that I was a little different from most paramedics because I saw patients healed in my ambulance.

With a puzzled look he delivered his next question. "What do you mean healed?"

I told him a few stories about some of my patients who had been healed. Now he was even more curious. "Can you do anything about my headache?"

I asked how bad it was. He said it was very painful, about eight out of ten. I placed my hand on his head and commanded the pain to leave in the name of Jesus then I asked how he felt.

"A little better," he said.

I put my hand on his head again and commanded the pain to leave then asked how he felt.

"A lot better."

I did it one more time and he said, "It's gone... completely gone." He was smiling from ear to ear. "Jesus just healed you."

"You're a Christian aren't you?" He asked.

"Yes, I am."

"That's what I thought. You know, I only have one problem with the way you Christians see Jesus. He was a good man and all, but He wasn't God. The Bible even says no man has seen God at any time. But Jesus was seen by the multitudes. So how could He possibly be God?"

"Look Maurice, I don't want to argue about religion. God healed your headache because He loves you. The healing is proof of that. God can heal the bleeding inside of you and that's my main concern right now. Can I pray for that to be healed?"

"Yeah, no problem man. Go ahead."

I placed my hands on his abdomen and commanded the bleeding to stop and for his kidneys to be healed. In the middle of praying it occurred to me to share the story about the experience Bonnie Jones had, where she was taken to a warehouse in heaven that was filled with spare body parts. She was told that the organs could be put inside people on earth who needed new ones.

When I was done declaring healing over him, he turned to me and said, "I want to tell you something. When I was comatose for two weeks, I wasn't unconscious. I was awake. And I had a very strange thing happen to me. During the time that I was in a coma I was in one of those warehouses like the one you mentioned and someone was with me. I didn't see them. I don't know who it was, but I felt comforted when I was with them. The one who was with me kept saying I would be okay. They said everything would work out. They told me my journey was not done. I had an assignment that must be completed."

We talked about the experience. I suggested that it was a near death experience like many that I'd read about and that the one who was with him was the Spirit of God. He didn't argue. Nothing in his knowledge of Islam could explain the experience. I told him a little bit about the Holy Spirit in the short time we had left. We arrived at our destination and moved him to his ICU bed. I gave report to the nurse and left out the fact that his headache was healed.

I learned so much on this transport. My view of Muslims was destroyed, but I'm working on a new one. I wrongly assumed I wouldn't be able to pray with this man, but he allowed me to pray. Actually, most Muslims love prayer and that was something I had never considered. What Maurice needed was someone to love him the way Jesus loves and heal him the way Jesus heals. It occurred to me that we often think people of other faiths have never had any true spiritual experiences or encounters with God. My new friend had a profound heavenly experience most of us will never have, this side of heaven. What he needed was someone he trusted to give him an interpretation of it. I was grateful that I'd been able to build a bridge of trust with him that day.

∞

Two days after transporting Maurice, I went to the ICU to check up on him. He gave me permission to tell his story, but we agreed to change his name. We talked for quite a while and laughed a lot. When I asked what the doctors found on examining him for bleeding, he told me that they ordered all the usual tests—both endoscopy and abdominal scans—and found no signs of bleeding. They were sending him home without surgery. He allowed me to pray for healing of his kidneys again.

Crystals, Magic Spells or Jesus?

THE NURSE MOTIONED FOR ME to leave the patient's room. I followed him into the hallway. He wanted to give report away from our patient and her family. She was admitted to the emergency department a few hours earlier for a severe headache. She had recently been diagnosed with breast cancer. Her head CT showed a new frontal lobe mass, which would likely be another tumor. She was being transferred to a larger hospital that had the capability of neurosurgery. I nodded and walked back into her room.

"Hi Paula. We're here to transfer you to Tacoma General. Are you ready to go?"

"I think so," she said slowly as she pulled her blonde hair away from her face with one hand, while shielding her eyes from the fluorescent light with the other.

"The nurse said you have a pretty bad headache. Is there anything else going on?"

"My gut is killing me."

I introduced myself and my partner and explained the transfer process. Having just transported Maurice who was healed of a headache, I felt this was another opportunity to demonstrate God's power and love.

"Paula, my plan is to have you feeling a whole lot better before we get where we're going."

She smiled. "So what do you have… some kind of crystals or magic spell for me?"

I smiled. "No, I don't do the crystal or magic spell thing. Let's just say pain and sickness don't like me very much."

After we had her loaded in the ambulance, I shared a few stories with her about people who had been healed—including what happened with Maurice. She was interested in hearing more, but it was a short trip so I had to get to work.

"Paula, would you like to be healed?"

"If you think you can make my headache go away, that would be great."

I placed my hand on her forehead. "Headache I command you to leave now in the name of Jesus. Spirit of pain, get out. So how do you feel now?"

"Better."

"Okay. Let's try it again. Pain I command you to leave in the name of Jesus. I command Paula's brain to be completely healed."

"How do you feel now?"

"It's a lot better," she said smiling.

I did it a third time and asked how she felt.

"It's gone."

"Are you serious or are you just saying that?"

"No, I'm serious, it's completely gone."

"So now it's time for me explain what's going on here. God just healed your headache because He loves you. If He healed that, He'll heal you completely."

"What about my stomach?"

"Let's pray again."

I placed my hand over her stomach. "Father I thank you for your power and love. I bless your continued work of healing in Paula. I command all pain to leave. I command spirits to go now in the name of Jesus."

Again I asked how she felt.

"It's not as bad."

"Lord you don't do anything halfway. I thank you for healing her headache and I know you want to heal her stomach. Pain get out now in the name of Jesus."

I asked once more how she felt.

"I think it's gone."

"Okay. I guess we have one last thing to pray over. Would you like that breast cancer to be gone?"

"I sure would."

I had her place her hand where the breast cancer was and I placed my hand on top of hers. I put my other hand on her forehead. "Cancer

I command you to leave now in the mighty name of Jesus. All sickness and disease leave now and do not return." When I was done I told her to close her eyes and rest until we got to our destination.

Her daughter, who was riding along, had streams of tears running down her cheeks. I love how the power of God moves the hearts of people. We arrived at Tacoma General and whisked her to the ICU, where we transferred her and I gave report. This time I told the nurse that her headache and abdominal pain were mysteriously gone. Before we left I bent down and whispered in Paula's ear, "God loves you."

∽

Two days later I went to the hospital to check up on Paula and I found her daughter and her mother coming off the elevator. The surgery to remove the brain tumor was a shorter procedure than expected and it went well. Paula was having an MRI when I stopped by so I didn't get to see her. Her family was grateful that a paramedic would take time to pray for her.

Casino Willys

IT WAS A HOT SUMMER day, so I decided to take the family to a car show. We love old cars. My dad took me to antique car shows and racetracks when I was a boy. He built hot rods with his brothers in the 1950s. One of his cars was a 1935 Ford five-window coupe. He and his friends put studded tires on their hot rods in the winter and raced them across frozen lakes. (And they say firefighters are crazy for going into burning buildings.)

My dad taught me a lot about fixing cars. I've never made a serious attempt to restore one, but my wife and I have a dream of one day restoring an old piece of American cast-iron. I saw a few cars that were for sale at the show, but they were just a *little* out of my price range.

As we rode the shuttle van from the parking lot to the casino, where the show was being held, I talked with my wife about who might get healed while we were there. I can't help it. I love seeing people healed and watching God on the move.

As we walked up and down between rows of beautifully restored classics, I was looking for someone with a cast, splint, or immobilizer. I'm not gonna lie. The 1941 Willys had my attention for a while. It was for sale, but I wasn't buying.

My daughter and I were having fun looking at the cars together, when I saw a woman limping through the crowd wearing a leg immobilizer. I thought I'd found the person who would be healed that day. We tried to make our way through the crowd to catch up to her, but she was walking toward the main entrance of the casino and before we could get there, she vanished inside. Rats!

After a few hours in the hot sun, some of my family took refuge in the beer tent. My daughter and I found shade in the food tent next door. After a bite to eat, I joined the rest of the group in the beer tent. We talked about the cars we'd seen. I pointed out the purple and yellow Willys to my wife and told her it was for sale. When I turned around to find another car to show her, I saw the woman with the leg immobilizer sitting at a table directly behind me.

I got her attention and introduced my family, then asked about her injury.

"Can you tell me what happened?"

"I feel really stupid. I was riding my moped and I crashed it in the ditch. I tore some of the ligaments in my knee and one of the tendons. It's pretty messed up."

I told her about some of the healing stories we'd seen. "Hey, can I pray for your leg to be healed?"

"Sure. That would be cool."

"How bad is the pain right now on a scale from one to ten?"

"I'd say it's about a five."

I placed my hand on her knee. "I command ligaments and tendons to be healed right now in the name of Jesus. Spirit of pain leave."

"Do you feel anything going on in there right now?"

"As soon as you started praying I felt tingling."

"Tingling is good. Okay Lord, you don't do anything halfway. Let's get this leg completely healed. I command all swelling and pain to leave right now, in the name of Jesus. How does it feel now?"

"Wow. That's amazing," she said as she felt her knee. "The pain is completely gone."

I looked at her and asked, "You're a Christian aren't you?"

"Yes I am," she said proudly. "Thanks so much for praying for me."

As I left the beer tent to meet up with my daughter, she immediately directed my attention to a girl about ten years old sitting in a wheelchair with a soft cast on her leg. My daughter was grinning from ear to ear. I went over and introduced myself.

"Why is your leg in a cast?"

Her grandmother explained. "Brittany tore the ligaments in her ankle."

I pointed to the woman who had just been healed and said, "Do you see that lady over there? She had the same kind of injury you have. She was just healed when I prayed for her. Would you like to be healed too?"

She nodded her head with a smile.

"On a scale from one to ten, if one is a mosquito bite and ten is the worst pain you can imagine, how bad is the pain right now?"

"About a three."

I placed my hand near her ankle without touching it. "Spirit of pain I command you to leave in the name of Jesus. Ligaments be healed. Okay Brittany, do you feel anything happening?

"Yes, it feels weird. Like tingling."

"On a scale from one to ten how much does it hurt right now?"

"I'd say one."

Then, I decided to do something a little more dramatic. I had seen another believer do this, but had never tried it myself. I pointed my finger at her ankle, like I was holding a Holy Spirit gun that would kill the pain. When I said, "BANG," she flinched. Then she said, "Hey, how did you do that? It's all better!"

"I didn't do anything. Jesus did it."

Brittany's grandmother took my hand and thanked me then turned to the girl. "You know dear, when you were a few years younger we prayed for some of your friends in Sunday school and they were healed just like you were."

"Thanks for letting us pray for you, Brittany," I said. "We'd better get going. I'm sure my wife is wondering where we are."

All the cars we saw were once just average cars for their age. They were a little rusty, a little worn out, dripping oil, and not running like they should. Someone came along and purchased them. But in that purchase, the goal was total restoration—lovingly replacing everything broken and making something beautiful.

The divine mechanic has the tools and know-how to fix every broken part of our lives. He has an endless supply of new parts to replace the bitter, failing ones we carry around. He's the master mechanic who wants us restored to wholeness.

Not as Drunk as You Suppose

My patient, a middle-aged man with long silver hair, and a swollen, dusky-red nose wore a flannel shirt and baggy pants that looked as though they hadn't been washed in weeks. The drafty, run-down shack that he lived in reeked of garbage, beer, and cigarette smoke. This morning it had one more odor: partly digested blood. There's just about nothing I hate more than the smell of blood that's been vomited after being in the stomach for a while.

He got up around three o'clock in the morning and began drinking. A short while later he began vomiting blood. His medical history was significant for emphysema, liver failure, and alcohol dependence. To make it worse, the alcohol had eroded either his esophagus or stomach, until blood vessels tore open and began to bleed. My new friend was a mess.

We loaded him in the ambulance and began transporting him. I tried to make small talk but he had a grumpy disposition and was in a lot of pain. Most of his comments were profanities. I really felt badly for him and I wanted to see God touch him in some way and maybe even heal him. In my spirit, I cried out for mercy and compassion. But I spoke not a word of it.

During the trip to the hospital he shoots me a look of amazement and suddenly says, "I feel really effing weird."

"What do you mean by weird?"

"I feel really high, like I'm stoned. But I never do drugs and it's not the booze. This is really effing weird!" As I watched, he began to giggle and smirk in the most amusing way. It was a short transport and we soon arrived at the hospital. I dropped him off and gave report without elaborating on what I'm sharing with you. I'm a little embarrassed to discuss what I think happened to him.

I'm a recovering Pharisee and maybe this is my treatment program. After God knocked the atheist out of me, He had to deliver me from a religious mindset that was offended by people getting "drunk in the spirit." I have to admit, I'm still a little uncomfortable about this at times.

The night before all this transpired some of my more charismatic friends came to my house and God proceeded to get us whacked in the Holy Ghost. People were laughing and falling on the floor in the joy of the Lord. It was a great time and I'll always remember that night fondly. But when my patient began to get giddy and happy, I realized it was God giving him a dose of the new wine.

Where do I go with this story and what does it mean?

I think it's safe to say that God loves everyone. Even mean old drunks. He loves us all and He wants us to be filled with life, health, and joy. And He's willing to go to extreme measures to do it... even getting someone drunk in the spirit in the back of an ambulance.

The eternal One heard an unspoken plea that mercy and joy should be extended to a miserable man and He gladly granted the request. That's my story and I'm stickin' to it.

Higher than Hi-Tech

WHAT DOES A BELIEVER DO when a co-worker is injured on the job? Here's what one person did:

Early in 2010, one of our ambulances was involved in an accident while on a call. The truck was severely damaged and both crew members suffered injuries severe enough to take time off work to recover. About nine months later, I was talking with one of the men from that crew about miracles and healing. Although he's a believer like me, he hasn't seen the miraculous healings that I have. As we got deeper into our conversation, he asked me a question that led to this discussion:

"You said you see a lot of people healed. What do you do that's different from everyone else who doesn't see consistent results when they pray?"

"I learned that begging God to heal people doesn't work. So instead of asking God to heal someone, I usually command healing to happen." I pretended his wrist was injured and demonstrated my method on his wrist. "If I wanted to get your wrist healed, I'd just place my hand on it and say, I command this wrist to be healed in the name of Jesus. I command tendons, ligaments, muscles, nerves and bones to be healed. I sometimes see spirits when I close my eyes and if I saw one I would tell it to leave. I learned that Jesus gave us the authority to do these things in His name."

"Remember the accident I was in last year? I'm still having pretty bad back pain from it, even though I went through physical therapy."

"Tell you what... I'll give you another demonstration. Let's get your back healed and you can watch how I do it."

So there we were in a parking lot, surrounded by ambulances, just a few blocks from a major hospital. All the high-tech medical equipment and education in town couldn't take away his back pain. I couldn't help but marvel at the irony of what was happening. I placed my hand on his back. "I command pain and inflammation to leave. I command discs, tendons, nerves, ligaments, and muscles to be healed, and bones to be aligned." I asked how he felt.

He twisted from side to side a few times. "Wow... it feels great!"

"Sweet. I love it when God does that. Well, I guess I better be going."

He gave me a hug. "Thanks man, I really appreciate your time and everything you taught me."

"My pleasure." I went inside, clocked out then came back out and got in my car. On the drive home I was awed by how easily God's power can be released through his kids.

∽

I followed up with my co-worker the week after we prayed and asked how his back was doing. He said it was great. He hiked the Skyline trail at Mt. Rainier the next day and told me about his plans to climb to the summit.

Gold Dust

IF YOU MADE A LIST of the most controversial topics in the present church scene, reports of "gold dust" showing up on people might be at the top of the list. In this story, I'll do my best to de-bunk some misconceptions, explain what this phenomenon really is, and share my own experiences. In order to address misconceptions about the appearances of gold dust let me first share a couple of illustrations.

Most prescription medications have side effects. Some of those side effects are allergic reactions, organ damage and in rare cases, death. Yet if these reactions are rare enough and the therapeutic effects are consistent enough in the general population, such medications are approved for use. Approval is based on the fact that a large number of people will benefit from the drug's use. The positive effects experienced by the majority outweigh the negative effects experienced by the minority.

Most nations in the world use some type of currency for trade. The use of currency has many benefits, but it has a few drawbacks. One drawback is counterfeiting. There will always be people looking to cheat the system for their own selfish reasons. Some people are obsessed with accumulating money and their love of money leads them to do things like counterfeiting currency. In spite of this, we haven't done away with the use of currency. The fact that a few people practice counterfeiting or that some people develop an unhealthy obsession over it, doesn't negate the legitimate use of currency.

I used these illustrations to highlight some problems in the way many of us look at things like the appearance of gold dust, manna, gemstones falling, clouds of God's glory and other unusual manifestations. Some of us have heard reports that people act strangely around these phenomena—even bizarrely. Some have accused people of coming under the influence of evil spirits. Others have heard that heavenly gemstones were fraudulently placed or that people tried to fake the appearance of gold dust. In evaluating these things, a number of questions should be asked:

1. If people have faked gold dust, does that mean that all appearances of gold dust are false?
2. If people have faked gemstones, are all such claims false?
3. If some people act strangely in these "glory clouds," does that mean everyone will act strangely and does it mean that the clouds aren't a real manifestation of God?

Going back to our first two illustrations, we can apply the same logic. The fact that some frauds exist doesn't mean the real thing doesn't exist. The fact that some people react strangely to a phenomenon doesn't mean everyone will, nor does it eliminate the possibility that people can receive great benefit from it. If we set our emotions and personal agendas aside, we could evaluate these things rationally and come to the truth about them.

Because I was an atheist for most of my life I still tend to view the supernatural with skepticism. I didn't believe in divine healing until a few years ago and my suspicion about manifestations such as gold dust has only recently begun to change. The change came when I started investigating these things for myself.

My wife and I were considering a possible relocation to Phoenix, Arizona and we decided to attend a conference being held there. The visit gave us a chance to check out the area. It also gave us the opportunity to check out some of these strange manifestations.

Patricia King was hosting an event called "The Ladder" conference. The guest speakers included Joshua Mills, Georgian and Winnie Banov, Todd White and Bobby Connor. We decided to go, but weren't sure what to expect. The night before we left I had a dream. In the dream, I traveled to Arizona to attend a conference, where I learned a great deal about the supernatural lifestyle of the kingdom of God. I came home and wrote about what I'd experienced and learned. In the dream, those who read the things I wrote were transformed by it.

The following day, we flew to Phoenix and attended the first day of the conference. The night before Todd White spoke, I had another dream. In the dream, Todd and I were on a large wooden floor. There were railings and barriers that had been set up in a large circle that we were inside of. We tore down, pushed over and dragged away all the barriers that had been put up until the floor was completely free of them.

In the first dream, God was confirming that I would learn and experience a lot of valuable things at the conference and that He wanted me to share them with you. In the second dream, God was illustrating the idea that we need to remove the barriers and restrictions we've placed on what God can do in our lives. The barriers have been put up by well-meaning people who feel that we need to be protected. God didn't erect these barriers—men did. God wants them removed so He has freedom to take us into the depths of His kingdom.

While we were at the conference we listened to Joshua Mills lead worship and encourage us to enter into a deeper relationship with the Lord. Not long after he began speaking, gold dust began to appear on him. It started as just a few specks, noticeable in the bright lights beaming down from above the platform, but after a while, it was more than just a few specks; it was a heavy dusting of a glittery gold dust-like substance.

Some people have suggested that these gold dust appearances are a fraud or that they're from the devil. The ones who think they are phony generally believe there are people nearby with containers of a gold dust-like substance, introducing it into the air to make it appear like a sudden manifestation of gold dust. That thought occurred to me as well, so I checked out the room and the crews.

The room we were in was about 50 feet long and 30 feet wide; an average size conference room with a flat ceiling about 18-20 feet high. There were no rafters, trusses, curtains, beams, ductwork or any sort of structures above the floor that would allow someone to spread gold dust from overhead. There were no fans or blowers in the room or anywhere nearby. I couldn't really see any ventilation ducts. The lights were pendants, hanging from the ceiling on heavy chains and these were the only things attached to the ceiling. I looked for possible ways that someone could have faked the gold dust and didn't find any plausible way it could have been done.

My wife is in charge of our checkbook. On this occasion, she heard God speaking to her about making a larger than usual donation. So when the offering bucket came around, she wrote out a check and dropped it in.

We were almost done with the session so we began to talk about where we would go for lunch. That's when I noticed a few specks of gold dust on my wife's face. Instinctively, we checked our hands and sure enough, tiny, almost invisible flecks of gold started to appear on her hands. We checked with those around us, but no one else had any on them.

We wanted to take pictures of it, so we walked outside to our car and got the camera. As we stood outside, it became obvious that the covering of gold dust was increasing. And now it was showing up on my hands, too. We took pictures and laughed at the fact that once again, God was demonstrating something just wonderful. So let me answer a few more questions some readers might have before we continue.

First, let me point out that if the gold dust phenomenon was a fake, the dust should have been more abundant inside, near the source of it and less abundant outside. But we experienced exactly the opposite. Very little dust appeared on my wife's hands inside, but when she came outside, more of it gradually appeared over the next fifteen minutes. I had none on me until we were outside for a few minutes.

Second, it seems that gold dust dissipates. The appearance of this substance is gradual, but once it reaches its maximum, a few minutes later it begins to disappear gradually until it isn't visible any longer. It's almost "wave-like" in how it comes and goes.

If the dust were some type of glitter or other man-made substance, it would be visible until it was removed and even then, you'd find it on the floor. But that isn't the case with heavenly gold dust. Generally a few minutes after it appears, it slowly vanishes. I have an explanation for why this happens. Many people wonder what the purpose is for the appearance of gold dust. I don't blame them for asking. I only hope they'll seriously consider the answer.

In his book, *Adventures in the Glory,* my friend Tom Calkins wrote about the time he went into a trance for about five hours during worship at a church. His body became as stiff as a board in his standing position. Physically, he didn't respond to his wife and others who were trying to find out what was going on with him. During these five hours, he went into the spiritual dimension and reveled in God's presence. He flew, floated and danced in a fine, gold substance that appeared exactly like the gold dust we're talking about.

The particles of gold came over him in increasing and decreasing waves. The amount of particles was never constant; it was always increasing or decreasing, much like waves of the ocean. There was always movement. As the particles became more abundant, with an increasing wave, his joy also increased. As the particles decreased, his joy decreased. But the most important thing Tom felt while in the waves of gold particles was the all-consuming, indescribable, passionate love that God has toward him. It was like nothing he'd ever experienced or imagined. At one point, Tom saw a large being; it appeared beside him. The being encouraged him to play and have fun in the waves of gold particles. The being himself seemed to become more brilliant when the intensity of particles increased and dimmed somewhat as the number of particles decreased.

As the particles decreased, almost to the point that there were none, Tom became frightened. In a desperate reaction, he wrapped his arms around the being standing beside him and the two of them began to move. They moved to a place where the wave of particles was increasing again. In a revelation that came about a year later, God explained the experience to Tom. While sleeping one night, God took him up into a heavenly perspective of that experience. He saw it the way God saw it and the Lord explained it to him:

The particles that he saw were the presence of God. His presence (or glory if you prefer) looks like particles of gold. The waves of particles are due to the fact that God's presence is always moving. He told Tom that His presence is always moving and so is all of creation. All the particles of the universe are in constant motion. God's glory moves in endless waves and always has since the beginning of time. It's His nature.

Tom's joy was because of the increase of God's presence upon him. That's how His presence works on our spirit; it brings increasing joy. When His presence decreases, so does our joy. The being that appeared beside Tom was the Holy Spirit. In the spirit realm every spirit has substance. They only lack substance in the natural realm. Tom's reaction to fear was to hold on to the Spirit of God, which is always a good move.

When the wave of glory decreased, the Holy Spirit moved him to a place where it was on the increase and once again, his joy increased. God's presence, because it moves in waves, is always increasing somewhere and always decreasing somewhere. God told Tom, "If you really want to experience my presence, find out where my presence is increasing and meet me there."

Some of my friends are fond of saying, "I'm not waiting for a move of God, because God isn't stuck." If they only knew how true that was. God isn't stuck and He never has been. He's always moving somewhere.

So what is the purpose of gold dust?

Well first, it isn't really gold dust so maybe we should stop calling it that. It's God's manifested presence, which happens to resemble particles of gold.

What's the purpose for it? What purpose does God have in making His presence come near to us?

To bring us joy, peace, love, healing and revelation. Perhaps a lot more, but that's enough for me. With all the war, hatred, addiction, anger and pain in the world, imagine what it would be like if the glory of the Lord covered the earth and its inhabitants reveled in His love, if only for a day.

It's part of God's nature to move, just as we move. "In Him, we live and move and have our being." He goes places to meet people who want to meet with Him.

One thing God told Tom was that it was his response to the sensation of heat on his arm during worship that made the experience happen. When he felt the sensation of heat on his arm, Tom's response was, "Is that you, Lord?" Sensing God's presence coming near and desiring to meet with Him is what opened the door to the encounter. God is looking for us to respond to His prompting. He loves us deeply and allowing us to be in His presence is how He shows us love.

The Bell Ringer

IT WAS A SUNNY BUT cold afternoon and I was at the grocery store to pick up a few things for dinner. A woman volunteer in a wheelchair sat at the entrance to the store ringing her Salvation Army bell as a blur of humanity passed before her eyes. A handful of coins plinked in her bucket. The bell rang again.

At the end of my workday I breezed through Safeway and quickly found a roasted chicken and a bag of coffee. The woman who ground my coffee asked, "Are you ready for Christmas?"

I gave her a smile. "I wish I was ready. Unfortunately, I still have a little more shopping to do."

I grabbed my coffee and headed to the checkout. I made small talk with the woman at the counter as she scanned my items. People came and went in a hurry, but the lady ringing the bell was still on my mind.

Peter and John went to the temple one afternoon to take part in the three o'clock prayer service. As they approached the temple, a man lame from birth was being carried in. Each day he was put beside the temple gate, the one called the Beautiful Gate, so he could beg from the people going into the temple. When he saw Peter and John about to enter, he asked them for some money.

Peter and John looked at him intently, and Peter said, "Look at us!" The lame man looked at them eagerly, expecting some money. But Peter said, "I don't have any silver or gold for you. But I'll give you what I have. In the name of Jesus Christ of Nazareth, get up and walk!"

Then Peter took the lame man by the right hand and helped him up.

And as he did, the man's feet and ankles were instantly healed and strengthened. He jumped up, stood on his feet, and began to walk! Then, walking, leaping, and praising God, he went into the temple with them. All the people saw him walking and heard him praising God.
(Acts 3:1-9 NLT)

Two thousand years later, I was standing before a crippled woman sitting at a gate asking for money. The irony of the situation hit me like a snowball in the face. I took her hand and asked her name, then asked why she was in the wheelchair. She smiled and told me about the problems she had with her hip. She had an injury that couldn't be repaired surgically and it was too painful for her to stand so she accepted the wheelchair as her fate.

More people came and went from the store. Children dropped their coins in her bucket. She rang the bell and smiled.

"Earlier today I prayed with a woman who had a back injury. She was completely healed. Would you like me to pray for you?"

"That would be wonderful," she said with a cheerful smile.

I placed my hand on her hip. "I command spirits of pain to leave. I command ligaments, muscles and tendons to be healed in Jesus' name."

I asked what she felt.

"I can feel something going on in my hip. It feels like tingling."

I prayed a second time. "Pain I command you to leave. Ligaments, tendons, bones, muscles and cartilage, be healed in Jesus' name."

I asked again how she felt.

"I can still feel the tingling, but my pain is much less than it was before."

I prayed one more time and asked how she felt. "I can't feel any pain," she said with a smile.

"Maybe you could get up and see how it feels when you're standing. I'd like to see you test it out a little bit."

She got up from the wheelchair and shifted her weight from side to side, trying to make the pain come back, but it wouldn't return. She was healed. With a smile of gratitude she hugged me.

I spent some time telling her what to expect in the coming days. I encouraged her to resist relying on the wheelchair again and also warned her that the pain might return. "Rebuke the pain and command it to leave. Don't take it back." I shared with her about the nature of spiritual warfare and suggested that the enemy may try to convince her she wasn't healed. "Stand on your healing and believe you are healed."

Before I left I gave her a big hug and dropped the largest bill I had in her kettle. "Merry Christmas!"

She smiled back and rang her bell one more time.

The Waiting List

WHAT CAN YOU DO WHEN surgery to repair a structural problem in your spine fails?

On a winter call in 2010, we took an elderly man home from the hospital. He had terminal metastatic cancer of the spine that had spread to multiple organs. When we got to his home we were met by his family. His daughter wanted to help us lift him into bed but she couldn't. She had a severe back injury. My partner and I moved him over with ease then I asked his daughter about her back.

She sustained a crushed vertebra in a car accident years ago. Typically, the damaged bone is repaired surgically with bone grafts. Metal plates or rods are attached to stabilize it further. Unfortunately, many patients suffer severe pain daily after this procedure. She was one of those cases. She was on the waiting list for a vertebral implant—a device that replaces the damaged bone. It's used with a bone graft to fuse the vertebrae together.

I decided to use a straightforward approach with her, so I said, "I was wondering if you'd like to be healed."

"If it doesn't hurt I might consider it," she replied. "What do you have in mind?"

"Oh nothing painful. Just a little demonstration of power."

"I don't know. Sounds kinda scary to me."

"It's easier to show it than it is to explain it. Don't you trust me?"

"Why don't you just tell me what you want to do?"

"Look I promise it won't hurt at all. In fact, you're probably going to feel a lot better when I'm done. I promise not to hurt you. Can I just place my hand on your back?" After thinking for a moment, she gave in and allowed me to try to get her healed. I placed my hand on the middle of her back. "I command this back to be healed in the name of Jesus. Holy Spirit bring your power upon her. All bones, be healed right now."

With a huge smile that soon turned to laughter she said, "I just love my Holy Ghost friends!"

"What do you feel?"

"Just the presence of God."

"Spirit of pain I command you to leave. Spine be healed." I asked again how she felt.

Twisting back and forth at the waist she said, "I can't feel any pain." She bent down and touched her toes and said all the pain was gone. She wrapped her arms around me and gave me a big hug and thanked me.

"Can you pray for my dad?" We knelt down beside his bed and prayed for healing. I gave her some information about how to keep the pain in her back from returning. She thanked us and we left.

It's my heart's desire that all believers learn how to pray with authority for the hurting people around them. Nearly everywhere I go there are people who need the great physician's healing touch. Some are on the waiting list, hoping for man's best invention as a remedy for their chronic pain. Jesus is so much better at healing than we are.

A Meeting With the Boss

ONE OF THE BIGGEST FEARS I had about praying for my patients was that someone would complain to my manager and I would be given an ultimatum to either stop praying or lose my job. In the U.K. many people have been fired from their jobs for praying with customers or talking with them about God. We have a little more freedom here in the U.S., but prayer in the workplace is not universally accepted and many people are vehemently opposed to it. My fear was that I would run into someone who was hostile to prayer and they would choose to make an example of me.

One day I transported a man to a hospital who was depressed and suicidal. After helping him to the bed in the emergency department I asked if he would like me to pray with him. He said he would, and I prayed that God would encourage him during this difficult time. Later that week I was called into my manager's office and asked to answer an accusation that had been brought against me. A complaint was filed by an emergency department nurse who saw me praying with the depressed man. She thought I was attempting to proselytize him and filed a complaint with her supervisor who passed along the grievance to my manager. That which I feared most had come upon me. My manager, Scott, asked me to explain exactly what it was that I was doing with regard to praying for my patients.

"So here's the deal Scott... one day not too long ago God asked me to pray for my patients and said that if I did He would heal them. I've tried to be obedient and I've been praying with some of the people I transport. Strangely enough, some of them have actually been healed.

MY CRAZIEST ADVENTURES WITH GOD — Volume 1

But I don't make it a habit to proselytize people. God didn't ask me to make converts. He asked me to pray for my patients. I always ask permission before I pray and if someone says 'no thank you' that's the end of the discussion. The man I prayed with the other day was depressed and suicidal. All I did was ask if I could pray with him and he welcomed it. So I prayed that God would encourage him and that was it. I'm not sure why the nurse thought I was trying to proselytize him."

Scott replied, "Well sir, I had to do a lot of research to determine the company's position on this matter. It seems that no one has ever been caught praying with a patient or at least not to where it generated a complaint. I checked all the company policies and procedures and consulted with all the regional managers and no one could point to anything that actually restricts employees like you from praying with your patients." He smiled and paused for a moment to let it sink in, then continued. "As far as I'm concerned you can keep praying for people but you need to realize that we must keep our customers happy… all of them. Even ER nurses who don't like this stuff. So I would ask two things of you: First, make sure you ask permission, and always respect the patient's wishes. Second, try to keep it confined to the back of the ambulance so people can't make trouble for us."

"Yes sir. I understand. Is there anything else?"

"No, that will be all."

Not long after this incident I had a dream that portrayed the situation from a different perspective.

In the dream, I was on the run, hiding from an enemy who was trying to find me and kill me. I walked along a road beside a wooded area. After walking for a while I went into the woods and met up with a group of soldiers who were wearing combat uniforms. I became one of them and we carefully made our way through the woods without being detected by the enemy. We came to a house and went into the basement. From a window we watched a large group of soldiers on a football field performing a musical number from a hit Broadway play called, "M-1". They went about executing perfect formations while singing songs and occasionally firing their rifles.

The scene then changed to a house. I was with a woman I don't know and I was in the house for a couple of days. I slept on a folding cot inside a screened porch. The woman slept next to me on her own cot. One night while I was sleeping the phone rang and I answered it. The person who called was pretending to be a friend, but I knew it was my enemy. I looked out the window of the screened porch and saw a sniper on a hillside about a half-mile away. He was ready to shoot me. The sniper was the person on the phone. He was trying to verify my location, but I told him I was somewhere else. The woman next to me didn't know what was going on. I knew the sniper was going to try to shoot me in a few seconds, so I yelled out "SNIPER!" As I did I rolled off the cot onto the floor just as a round came through the screen toward me. But it missed me. I taunted the enemy telling him he was a crappy sniper and he missed. Suddenly we were under fire from automatic weapons and many rounds came through the wall. When there was a break in the gunfire I taunted the enemy again telling him he couldn't hit me even with an automatic weapon.

I left the house and decided I needed to find a safer place. I went to a large hospital and put on a pair of scrubs so I would blend in with the other employees. I was in the hospital for several days. Sometimes I would wear a surgical mask to hide my face because I knew the enemy was still looking for me. I pretended to be an employee and at night I slept in a doctor's suite on the top floor of the hospital. Some days I pretended to be working in housekeeping, some days I pretended to be a technician in the emergency or operating room. My plan was to avoid coming into contact with the enemy. All the time that I was in the hospital I felt safe. There didn't seem to be a direct threat to me as long as I didn't draw attention to myself.

I interpreted the dream as a parable about the spiritual warfare I was experiencing. The soldiers I met up with and joined were other believers. God wanted me to realize I was now engaged in a battle against a real enemy and that I was not alone. The performance we watched represented the power of worship as warfare. The sniper was the enemy, who was trying to take me out. The hospital represented my workplace and ministry. I never actually experienced any direct threat in the workplace. The key was to look like everyone else, but to function in the gifts God asked me to operate in, without drawing attention to myself.

During the five years I've been praying with my patients I would estimate that I've prayed with over three thousand people on duty. There has only been one complaint, which helped establish the fact that my employer would support me as long as I prayed in a way that wouldn't cause problems for them. In all that time I can only remember five or six patients who declined my offer to pray with them.

Undercover Work

WE BROUGHT A FREQUENT FLIER to the emergency department. Not long ago, my partner transported him three times in one day. This time he called 911 for a headache. As my partner steered him to the waiting room, I noticed a friend who works as a receptionist with her arm in a sling. My partner gave report on our patient. I pulled up a chair and began asking about her injured arm.

"Hey... that looks kinda painful. What the heck did you do?"

Gabriela's brown eyes peered at me through a curtain of long black hair that hung over her face. Tossing her hair aside she said, "I feel kinda stupid. I fell in the shower and I haven't had an x-ray yet because I know they're gonna tell me it's broken and I really don't want to have surgery."

"Well maybe you won't need surgery. You *could* let me pray for it to be healed instead."

"Are you crazy? I'm at work! I can't do something like that now."

"I've been doing this for a while now and I've learned how to get people healed in a way that doesn't draw attention. No one will know what's going on."

She agreed. I placed my hand on her elbow, and very quietly, with my head down, commanded the pain and inflammation to leave and the spirit of pain to go and never return. I asked if she felt anything.

"Tingling."

"You're being healed."

"Are you serious?"

"Yup."

I repeated the process one more time and asked what she felt. She described a sensation of warmth inside her arm, which was strange because she had an ice pack inside the sling. "That's the power of God healing you," I said with a smile. We talked for a few more minutes. I explained that the pain might return and encouraged her to stand firmly in faith on her healing and if any pain returned to command it to leave.

An hour later we were at another hospital, transferring a man to a nursing home. His daughter-in-law was with him. She was sitting in a wheelchair. I asked why she was in the wheelchair. "Because my ex-husband has an anger management problem and he did something that gave me a spinal cord injury."

I didn't ask for details. I could see she didn't want to talk about it. I knelt down so I could see her at eye level and told her about my friend who had just been healed at the other hospital. "Would you like to be healed?"

She hesitated. "I have people praying for me, but I have a lot of problems with my right foot. I still can't bend it." She lifted up her right leg and displayed her limp foot and how she couldn't move it.

"Can I ask what your name is?"

"Sure. It's Susan."

"Susan, I see miracles happen almost every day. God can fix that. Can I pray for you?"

With uncertainty in her voice she said, "Go ahead."

I placed my hand on her right leg. "I command Susan's spinal cord to be healed in the name of Jesus. Legs I command you to be strengthened right now. Spirits of disease and sickness, I command you to leave in the mighty name of Jesus. Nerves be healed, muscles be healed, and tendons be healed in Jesus' name." I asked if she felt anything.

"Tingling... mostly in my right leg."

"You're being healed."

"Really?"

"Really, really."

I prayed one more time and told her she was on her way to being healed. I gave her some instructions on how to maintain her healing over the long haul. She thanked me and watched as we loaded her father-in-law on the gurney. As we left, I took her hands in mine one more time and told her, "You are healed. God is faithful."

I'm Not a Stalker

I WENT WITH MY DAUGHTER to the grocery store. I'm not deliberately trying to influence her in the direction of healing. It just sort of happens. Leaving the store, I noticed a middle-aged woman limping toward the parking lot. I felt like I heard the Holy Spirit say, "Go get her."

I approached, gave her my best smile and asked why she was limping.

"I don't know you sir and I'm not sure that's any of your business."

"I'm a paramedic. I work in Tacoma. I'm not crazy and I'm not a stalker. I just like to see people blessed by the healing power of God. You can ask my daughter... honest, lady!"

"You're a paramedic huh? Do you always go around asking strangers about their personal problems?"

I was a little embarrassed. She didn't brush us off completely, but she wasn't exactly welcoming us into her life. I looked at the flowers sitting happily in their pots at the entrance to the store. "Look ma'am. I don't always do this with strangers. I try to obey the Lord when I feel He wants me to talk to someone."

"Well I'm sorry if it seems like I'm being defensive. I'm just not used to people I don't know asking me things like that."

"I'm sorry. I know this must be terribly awkward for you."

She looked at my daughter. "You seem like a nice girl. Does he always do this kind of stuff?"

My daughter smiled. "Well actually, yes he does. We do pray for a lot of strangers."

We were creating a little bit of a scene at the entrance to the store. I wanted to take the conversation somewhere else where she wouldn't feel like people were listening. "Why don't we walk to your car and talk about it on the way there?"

She limped pathetically toward her car and let me push her cart. As she walked I could see that it was her knee that was giving her trouble. She couldn't bend it.

"Looks like your knee is in pretty bad shape. Can I ask what's wrong with it?"

"Well if you must know, I have a torn meniscus and I need surgery. And because I don't have insurance right now I can't afford the surgery. But if I don't have the procedure and my knee gets worse I may not be able to work. So I'm in a bad spot right now and I'm not very happy about it."

"May I please try to get your knee healed? What will it hurt if I just try?"

"Well it looks like you aren't going to leave me alone until I say yes, so go ahead."

I placed my hand on her knee. "I command this knee to be healed in the name of Jesus. I command the meniscus to be healed. Inflammation leave right now!" I asked how she felt.

She bent down and felt her knee. "It feels a little better."

I placed my hand on her knee again. "Meniscus I command you to be healed right now. Pain and inflammation I command you to leave."

I asked again how she felt.

"Well what do you know? It doesn't hurt at all." She looked at me like I was crazy and asked, "Are you for real?"

"Jesus is more real than you know and He's the one who healed you. He loves you and He has a great plan for your future."

I asked if she had any other conditions I could pray for. She let me pray for back pain and high blood pressure. We talked for a while about the goodness of God. She gave me a hug and we left her with a huge smile on her face.

I learned an important lesson that day. This woman had a lot of stress over her injury and my insistence on talking about it probably brought up worries she didn't want to think about. There's a fine line we must walk when dealing with the personal problems of a stranger. If you become too aggressive, it's harder to create an environment of trust. I had to let the trust develop at her pace. So I patiently talked with her about her concerns to help put her at ease. Of course, I think it also helped that I had my lovely daughter along to back me up!

The Wrong Rotator Cuff

ONE OF THE HAZARDS OF surgery is accidentally removing the wrong body part. There are thousands of cases of "medical misadventures" every year: patients who have the wrong kidney removed, the wrong leg amputated or just about any other mistake you can think of. Understandably, when things like this happen, patients are never happy about it.

One day I prayed with a sweet 94-year-old woman who was admitted to a hospital for nausea and back pain. During her stay she developed short pauses in her heart rhythm. There was a possibility that the short pauses in her rhythm would become long pauses or that her heart would stop beating altogether. Her doctor arranged to have her transferred to a larger hospital where she would have a pacemaker implanted.

She was the sweetest little old lady. I told her I'd adopt her as my grandmother if she wanted another grandson. She didn't want anyone to make a fuss over her and she smiled about everything. During the transport I put the blood pressure cuff on her left arm. "Oh, please be careful with my arm. I have a torn rotator cuff and frozen shoulder and it hurts."

Because her arm was too small for a regular adult cuff, I gently wrapped the pediatric cuff around her upper arm. When I was done taking her blood pressure I gently took the cuff off. "You know... I pray with a lot of my patients and a fair number of them are healed. How would you like to have that frozen shoulder healed?"

"Oh, that would be wonderful!" She told me about Jesus and the things He'd done in her life. I gently touched her left shoulder. "I command pain and inflammation to leave. Spirits of pain get out. Muscles, ligaments, tendons, bones and nerves, in the name of Jesus I command you to be healed." I don't like "formulas" very much, but this is one I routinely use for healing orthopedic injuries. I rarely deviate from it, unless the Holy Spirit shows me something different. I also learned that it's a good idea to command spirits to leave as a matter of protocol, even if I don't sense that a spirit is present. Most of the people I pray for who have sprains, strains, tears and fractures are healed this way.

I asked the Holy Spirit to come with His power and presence and I prayed over her shoulder three times. I also commanded her heart to be healed. After each time, I asked if she felt anything or if she could raise her arm. She didn't feel anything and couldn't lift her arm when I was done. I'll admit I was a bit puzzled. I really expected her to be healed. We continued the transport and I did my charting. Ten minutes later, just before we arrived at the destination hospital, she raised her right arm in surprise and said, "I can't believe it. My shoulder is healed! Praise God! It's a miracle!" Now I was really confused.

"Ma'am, I thought it was your left shoulder that had the torn rotator cuff and was frozen. That's the one I prayed for."

"Sonny, I didn't tell you this, but both my shoulders were frozen. I'm right-handed and this is the one that really needed to be healed. I don't care as much about my left shoulder." She was praising Jesus as we wheeled her into the hospital.

We took her to the cath lab and transferred her to the bed. I gave report to the nurse. Yes, I told them she was healed on the way. The gals in the cath lab have been hearing my stories. Maybe one day soon they'll have their own healing stories to share with me.

Ambushed

I HAD A BUSY DAY at work and I was pretty tired. When I got home my wife was having a conversation with our son in the living room. I sat with them and tried my best to follow what they were saying but I kept dozing off so I finally went to bed. My wife was tired, so she went to bed with me. As we lie in bed, we both felt led to pray for our friend Scott Buzzell who was battling Lou Gehrig's disease.

As soon as I was asleep, I had a dream. In the dream I was trying to empty my mind of distractions to hear the voice of God. He was giving me His heart for someone else and I was trying to discern what it was He wanted to give to them. The first thing He spoke to me about was "peace." I couldn't have been sleeping very long, but I immediately woke up and wrote down the dream. As I wrote it down on a note card, my wife who was still awake asked, "Did you have a dream?"

"Yeah. It was about hearing God's heart for someone. He wants to give them peace."

"Well I had a really strange thing that just happened. I was awake… or at least I thought I was awake, but I must have had a dream about giving Scott Buzzell a car seat. Or maybe it was a vision."

"That is strange, but we prayed for Scott before we went to sleep, so maybe it has something to do with that."

At this time my wife was working at a company that manufactured car seats. "We had a call at work today from the actor Charlie Sheen. He thanked us because the car seat he bought saved his kid from being injured in a car accident. We told him we'd send him a replacement

because the one he bought had been damaged in the accident."
"Well that's pretty cool." I replied.
"I can't sleep, honey. I have pain all over my body. I've been tossing and turning ever since we went to bed. It's driving me crazy." She looked toward the ceiling. "God, if there's some reason why you want me to be awake tonight would you please tell me what it is?"

She had been dealing with chronic pain for a long time. I prayed for her every night but it didn't seem to help. So once again I began praying for her pain to go away. Tonight I tried a different approach. "God let me have her pain. If it's possible for me to take her pain, I'll take it. Just let me have her pain. If it will remove it from her, let me take her pain and let her sleep tonight." I was tired and desperate. I begged God over and over to put her pain on me. A few minutes later I was asleep and had another dream. In this dream I was in an elevator going to various floors looking for someone or something, but I didn't know what it was I was searching for. At the end of the dream I was at a large shopping mall, it seemed like I might have been at a Macy's Department store. As I left the elevator, I woke up and said to myself, "I need to write this down."

Suddenly, I felt an evil presence surround me. I could feel many small sensations on my skin like the wings of birds brushing against me, or like a net of some kind being spread over me. In a few seconds I was unable to move my arms or legs. When I realized I was under a demonic attack, I knew I had to quickly speak against it in the name of Jesus. But as soon as this thought entered my mind, I felt my voice leaving me and I could no longer speak. The demon that had attacked me was preventing me from saying the words I knew I had to say. I tried to speak but could only mumble the words, "In Jesus' name, leave me, in Jesus' name, leave me." I was also rolling a bit from side to side, trying to get free from what was binding my arms and legs.

My wife was still awake and heard me mumbling something over and over. "Honey, what's happening?" She asked.

I kept mumbling, "In Jesus' name, in Jesus' name."

She could barely make out the words, "in Jesus' name" and knew I must have been under a spiritual attack. She instinctively yelled out, "Get away from him NOW in the name of Jesus!" Then she began praying in tongues.

The demonic presence left and I could move my body again. When I was able to talk, I blurted out, "What the hell was that?" But we both knew exactly what it was. In the past, my wife had suffered similar attacks. We spent some time praying against the forces of evil and sang a few verses of "Praise Adonai." Soon we felt peace and were able to sleep with no more attacks or dreams.

This encounter taught me a number of things. The first is that you should never ask God to take the pain or afflictions from someone and give them to you. It opens a door for the enemy to attack you. Instead of asking for their pain to be given to you, just keep believing that God wants them to be healed and stand in faith for their healing to manifest.

The second thing I learned is that when you begin to operate in power and authority and start to advance the kingdom of God, you become a greater threat to the kingdom of darkness. As the demonic world takes notice of your activities, it should not surprise you when you find opposition and harassment. All of this simply means you're beginning to make a difference and the enemy isn't happy about it. A World War II vet who flew bombing missions once said, "When you start taking flak it's a sure sign that you're over the target."

Lastly, after doing some research, I learned that attacks by paralyzing spirits like the one I encountered are extremely common and are reported in virtually every culture and have been since ancient times. Fortunately, these spirits tend to be easily repelled by merely speaking the name of Jesus.

You Came Back!

ONE EVENING WHILE NEARING THE end of my shift on the ambulance, I stopped at a grocery store to buy potatoes and onions for dinner. As I waited in a line at the checkout, I noticed the clerk rolling her head from side to side with a look of pain on her face.

"Good evening, sir," she said. "How are you doing tonight?"

"I'm doing pretty well. Just picking up some things for dinner. What's the deal with your neck pain?"

"Oh that," she said slightly embarrassed. "I've had it for a while, but I don't remember how or when it started."

"Would you like to be healed?"

"Why, are you a massage therapist?"

"Not exactly. I pray for a lot of people in grocery stores and many of them are healed."

"I'm sold!" She said excitedly.

But we had a problem. She had a line of customers waiting and I couldn't stay long. I gave her a card to my website and told her I'd be back soon to pray for her. I left the store with mixed feelings: glad for the opportunity to plant a seed of hope, but disappointed that I didn't get to pray with her. I came to work the next day and ended up at the same store again. As I approached the store, I met two men who were taking donations to help disabled veterans. I introduced myself and shared my admiration for what they were doing.

I noticed one of the men wore dark sunglasses, even though it was not a sunny day. Looking at him, I asked what kind of vision problems he had.

"How do you know about my eye problems?" He asked.

"People don't normally wear sunglasses on an overcast day unless they have something wrong with their eyes. Call it an educated guess."

"Well as a matter of fact, I have glaucoma in my left eye and I've had cataract surgery, but I really can't see anything out of it."

"Any chance I could pray for your eye to be healed?"

With a big smile, he said, "Sure."

I placed my hand on his shoulder. "Holy Spirit bring your presence and power to heal. Lord I ask you to fill him with your peace. Darkness I command you to leave. Eye be healed in Jesus' name. Glaucoma, I command you to leave right now." I asked how he felt.

Smiling and laughing he said, "I feel like all my anxiety just left and I feel that peace you were talking about. You know what? I think I can even see a little better, too."

"The peace you're feeling is the Holy Spirit. Can I pray for your eye again? I usually like to continue until I see more progress."

"Absolutely."

I placed my hand on his forehead near the eye that had glaucoma. "I command this eye to be healed right now. I command glaucoma to leave in Jesus' name. Holy Spirit, bring your power to heal. Okay, check out your vision again."

He reported that it was even better now.

I wanted to see if the woman with neck pain was working. "Hey guys, I really admire what you're doing. I need to go pray for someone else. It's been a real pleasure meeting you. God bless." I shook their hands and went inside the store and found the woman with neck pain at her check stand with a line of people waiting their turn. I saw another store employee and asked if he knew what time her next break was. It was coming up in 15 minutes, so I decided to wait. She saw me waiting and smiled, holding up one finger to let me know she'd be able to talk in a minute or two. After a few minutes she closed her check stand.

Walking toward me she exclaimed, "You came back!" I asked how she was feeling. "You came at the right time. I have a migraine headache and my neck and shoulders are killing me."

I wanted to give her hope that she could be healed, so I shared the first story in this book about the store employee who was healed of migraines. It worked; she was encouraged. We talked about that story as we stepped outside to find a place to pray away from all the activity in the store.

"Okay, so you have pretty bad pain in your neck and shoulders and a migraine headache. Anything else?"

"No, that about covers it."

I placed my hand on her shoulder. "Holy Spirit bring your presence. Spirit of pain I command you to leave in the name of Jesus. Headache leave now. Bones in the neck come into alignment. Ligaments, tendons and nerves be healed in Jesus' name." I asked how she felt.

"I feel great. My headache is completely gone."

"Are you lying? You can be honest with me. You're not going to hurt my feelings if you tell me you're not healed."

Smiling, she said, "I'm a big girl, and I'm being honest. My headache really is gone."

She still had a little pain between her shoulder blades so I placed my hand there. "Pain I command you to leave right now in the name of Jesus." I asked again how she felt.

She moved her shoulders up and down to see if she could make the pain come back. "It's completely gone now."

"Isn't God just amazing?" I asked.

With a knowing smile she said, "Yes, He is."

As we stood in front of the store, a bitter wind chilled our faces. We talked about the goodness of God, which she'd experienced many times. She knew the Lord well. Today's encounter was a further revelation of His deep love and mercy toward her.

"Well... I suppose I need to go back to my work," she said as she turned toward the store. My EMT partner napped peacefully in the front of the ambulance, oblivious to what had just happened. In the distance I heard the wail of a fire engine. Walking toward the rig I said to myself, "I guess I need to get back to work, too."

Chicken Strips and Wrist Immobilizers

One day while on duty, we paid a visit to a part of the city that my partner and I really like. Northeast Tacoma is a small, residential area perched on a hill overlooking the port of Tacoma. The view is nice, but the food is amazing. While killing time waiting for a call, we went to our favorite Shell station for fuel and food. I don't normally eat gas station food, but this gas station makes the best chicken strips in town. While my partner filled the ambulance fuel tank, I got lunch.

I went inside and ordered a 4-piece box of chicken strips. I noticed that the young woman with blonde hair who took my order was wearing a black immobilizer on her wrist.

"Here are your chicken strips, sir. Did you want any dipping sauce?"

"Do you have any barbecue sauce?" She grabbed two packets of barbecue sauce and handed them to me. "Carpal tunnel?" I asked, pointing to the immobilizer on her wrist.

"Yeah... and I hate wearing this thing,"

"How would you like to be healed?"

Using her fingers to gesture quotation marks in the air, she asked, "What do you mean by 'healed'?"

"I've prayed for a lot of people with carpal tunnel syndrome and many of them have been healed."

She looked at me, rolled her eyes and in a sarcastic tone said, "whatever." She was skeptical, which is understandable if you've never seen anyone healed at a gas station. But this wasn't my first barbecue. Before I paid for the food, I asked her to hold out her arm and she did.

"Can I pray for you?" I asked.

"Sure, if it makes you feel better."

I gave her a wry smile. "I feel fine. You're the one who's going to feel better." I placed my hand on the immobilizer. "I command this wrist to be healed in the name of Jesus. I command the spirit of pain to leave right now. Inflammation I command you to go." I asked if she felt anything.

"No, it still hurts."

I prayed again. "Spirit of pain, get out now in Jesus' name. Carpal tunnel be healed. Do you feel anything different?"

She tried to move her hand in a circle. "Nope, it still hurts."

I prayed a third time. "I command the carpal tunnel to be opened now in this wrist. Ligaments and tendons be healed in Jesus' name." I asked again if she felt any change.

"Nothing. It still hurts."

I told her that sometimes people get healed, though they don't feel any changes immediately. Sometimes they notice the symptoms go away the next day or even a week later. "I believe you're healed and I think you'll feel it soon. When you're healed, just know that God did it because He loves you." I thanked her and left with my chicken strips, which were awesome.

We went back to the Shell station about two weeks later for fuel. While my partner filled the tank, I went inside to get some of those yummy chicken strips. I saw the same woman behind the counter. She wasn't wearing the wrist immobilizer so I asked her where it was. With a smile she said, "I don't need it anymore, my wrist feels great."

"Now that you've been healed, let me tell you how to keep the pain from coming back. Healing is a little like warfare. There's this enemy out there who wants you to have that pain back. Jesus wants you to be healed. If the pain returns, just tell it to leave in the name of Jesus and keep believing you're healed."

"Okay, I'll remember that," she replied. "Hey, are you gonna get some chicken strips or not?"

"Of course I am! The chicken strips here are amazing. But not as amazing as Jesus."

How to Do Surgery in Your Sleep

I RECEIVED THE FOLLOWING MESSAGE from someone through Facebook on March 29, 2011:

Good morning to you! I have a special request. My Facebook friend (name omitted) an Administrator with me on our Intercessory Prayer Page sent me a message. She is very upset right now about her Pastor in her church whose only kidney is failing, not doing well. She is confused because she wonders why God didn't heal him when he gave up his blood pressure medications a couple of years ago and branched out in faith thinking he was "healed." I don't want to get into details but thought maybe if you would please "friend her" you could help her and pray for her Pastor as well. I told her a little bit about you and that we are friends. She will be looking for you I'm sure. I gave her my views on this, but I was following some of your posts, you are more blessed in this area than I, and you have the healing ministry. Love you Bro, and thank you!

I replied to her message and sent a friend request to the person she mentioned. That person accepted my friend request and asked for prayer for her pastor, explaining his situation:

He (the pastor) believed God two years ago to come off of his high blood pressure medication. God had healed him of cancer of the kidneys some 20 years ago and although he had one kidney removed because of the cancer, he refused chemotherapy and has been clean of cancer for over 20 years. When he got off his medicine cold turkey, we as members honored his faith but we also were very cautious and concerned about this move. He hung up his pill bottles on the wall to demonstrate his faith. Since that time, he had been having severe headaches and pain in other parts of his body but nothing major. He just kept claiming his healing and he declared that he would not get back on his medicine even if it cost him his life. Well, time went on and he never missed a beat and we all thought he was healed until he was suddenly hospitalized. The only kidney he has left is at 25% functional and his prostate is enlarged. I really want to believe God for a miracle for him today because it bothers me that he stepped out in faith but was not healed (obviously.)

I replied that I would pray for her pastor. So I prayed for him and then for a few others on my list that evening. That night I had a dream:

In the dream, I was with a man who needed a new kidney. He was an average looking man, but I could see he had a surgical opening in his side. The opening was clean, with no blood present. He beckoned me to come near him and put my hand in his side and try to find his kidney. I placed my hand in the opening in his side and moved around some of his organs to try to locate it. Then the dream ended.

I awoke and told my wife about the dream. We talked about it and tried to find an interpretation, but I didn't understand it. (I had completely forgotten about the pastor I prayed for the previous day who needed a new kidney.) That afternoon, the friend who asked me to pray for her pastor posted this on my Facebook page:

Praying Medic: I have a Praise Report! God has restored my Pastor back to health. He is to be discharged from the hospital tomorrow. Thank you for praying and thank God for your intense healing ministry. I've been reading your blog and learning a lot.

Two days later she sent me this private message:

Remember the one kidney that was severely damaged and operating at 25% and docs were talking dialysis and transplant? His wife told me this morning that when they checked his kidney again it showed it is now functioning at 100%!

Apparently, when you're working with God, even kidney surgery is easy. So easy you can do it in your sleep.

God Loves a Girl in Uniform

BEFORE MOVING TO ARIZONA IN 2011, I flew to Phoenix to take a paramedic test. On a Sunday morning I was sitting in the hotel lobby with my computer, browsing Facebook and having coffee. I noticed there were a lot of teenagers in the lobby wearing softball uniforms. It turns out there was a girls' softball tournament in town. A girl in uniform and her mother were sitting next to me. I heard the girl mention to her mother that she was having a lot of shoulder pain.

I turned toward the girl. "Hey... how would you like to be healed?"

She smiled. "And how would that happen?"

"I pray with a lot of people who are healed of different medical problems."

She said, "Sure!"

I moved my chair closer to their table and began asking questions. "How long have you had the pain in your shoulder?"

"A couple of weeks."

"How bad is the pain on a scale from one to ten, if ten is the worst pain you can imagine?"

"I'd say about a five."

I checked her range of motion then placed my hand on her shoulder. "I command the spirit of pain to leave in the name of Jesus. Inflammation get out now. Ligaments, muscles, bones, tendons and nerves, I command you to be healed." I asked if she felt anything different.

"It feels really warm, but it still hurts a little."

I placed my hand on her shoulder again. "Lord I thank you for the healing you've already done and I know you don't do anything halfway.

I believe you want her completely healed. I command this shoulder to be healed right now in the name of Jesus. Ligaments, tendons, bones, cartilage and nerves be healed." I asked again how she felt.

"It's a lot warmer now and the pain is almost gone." She was surprised at how quickly she had been healed. I talked with her and her mother for about 20 minutes. I shared some God stories and showed them my healing website on my computer then told them if they wanted to learn more about healing they should check it out. The girl's mother happened to be a paramedic. She's seen people healed in her church, but wanted to know why some people lose their healing.

I taught them what I knew about spiritual battles and why people seem to lose their healing. "If the pain comes back, don't receive it. Believe that you are healed and understand that the enemy is just trying to mess with you. Don't fall for it. Command the pain to leave the same way I did."

What I didn't know was that sitting at the next table there was another teenaged girl who had a friend with an injured shoulder. As I got up to leave, five girls, all wearing uniforms, approached me and asked if I could get their friend healed.

"Have any of you ever seen a miracle?"

They all said, "No."

"Well you're about to see a miracle today. If you let me pray for her shoulder, God is going to heal her." I looked around and it seemed like everyone in the lobby including the staff working behind the desk was looking on in anticipation as I explained what was about to happen. The injured girl came forward. I could tell she was nervous. "Hey, there's nothing to be worried about. Can I ask a couple questions before we get started?"

"Sure, I guess so."

"Can you tell me how you injured your shoulder?"

"It happened in a baseball game a couple years ago. It never really healed and it hurts most of the time."

"Okay... well this shouldn't take very long." I placed my hand on her shoulder. "Holy Spirit, bring your presence and power upon this girl. I command this shoulder to be healed in the name of Jesus. Ligaments, tendons, muscles, cartilage and nerves be healed right now." I asked if she felt anything.

"What do you mean?"

"I mean do you feel any different from how you felt a few minutes ago?"

"Well... I feel really warm and kind of tingly all over."

"That's the power of God healing you," I replied. I prayed a second time and asked the Holy Spirit to bring more of His power upon her then asked what she felt.

"Now my shoulder feels a lot better and I'm getting really hot... like all over." She began to giggle. It was obvious she was happy to feel God's presence touching her as she was being healed. Her friends looked on in amazement. I spent a few minutes explaining to the girls that anyone who is a disciple of Jesus can heal people like I did and I taught them about the spiritual battles involved in healing.

When I had answered all their questions, the girls left and went to their rooms. I opened a document on my computer and began writing up this story while it was still fresh in my mind. As I was writing, a woman approached me and asked if I was the one who healed the girls. I said I was. She had a question for me. "Do you think God would heal me of fibromyalgia and gluten intolerance?"

"I believe He would," I said.

It was the answer she was hoping for. She sat down next to me and three of her friends joined us. When she was ready for me to pray with her I placed my hand on her shoulder.

"Holy Spirit, bring your presence upon this woman. I release the healing power of the kingdom of heaven. Spirit of pain and spirit of trauma I command you to leave right now in the name of Jesus. Inflammation I command you to go." As I prayed she felt the power of God touch her and she began weeping tears of joy.

As I spoke to her about how much God loves her I couldn't help but marvel at how fast the good news of God's love travels. It's a message of power and love and it's one that nearly everyone wants to hear.

Only Skin Deep

AFTER LOSING HER BALANCE AND falling at home a couple of times, Terri took a tumble down the stairs and landed on her head. The head CT showed both subdural and subarachnoid hemorrhages. This would be a trauma transfer to a larger hospital for neurosurgery. I've never met anyone who was proud of the fact that drinking had destroyed their liver. Normally, it's a regret they must live with and most people would give anything if they could do it all over again. Terri had struggled with drinking for years and it took a severe toll on her 46-year-old body.

A nurse named Heidi helped me get Terri ready for the transfer. While Heidi acted as an IV pole, holding the bag of plasma as close to the ceiling as she could because gravity helps get it through the IV line faster, I asked if she wanted me to get a pressure infuser, so she could do more important things, like getting the paperwork together so we could hit the road. We fitted the c-collar on Terri so as not to rip the IV out of her neck and rolled her onto the hard backboard. I put a blanket on it first so it would be a little more comfortable.

As we loaded her into the rig, I thought about how I'm growing farther away from my comrades in how we see our patients. Just about everyone involved in her care (except Heidi) had a critical remark about how Terri lives her life.

Drunk. Loser. Psycho. Alcoholic. I looked at her and saw a broken-hearted woman, desperately in need of one person who believed in her. After getting her vitals and most of my charting done, I told her I saw a lot of people healed in the ambulance. "Terri, if you want me to pray with you, I would be honored."

With tears welling up in her eyes she softly said, "I'd really like that."

I placed one hand on her forehead and she gripped my other hand tightly in hers. "Bleeding I command you to stop right now in the name of Jesus. I release the healing power of the kingdom of God into Terri's body. Lord, show her your love and compassion."

As I spoke to her soul about God's great love and compassion for her, tears flowed like a river down her jaundiced cheeks.

"Lord, you did not bring Terri into this world so she could suffer. You aren't going to leave her this way. You have a glorious plan to redeem her life. I declare the goodness and mercy of God over you, Terri. I declare God's blessing and His hand of favor over you. I declare that by his stripes you are healed." As I declared God's goodness and protection over her, she gripped my hand even tighter. The yellow pigment of her skin and the bruises that covered her body only told part of the story.

"Thanks so much for praying for me. I know God loves me. I know He's there and I try so hard to do the right things. But I keep messing up. I want to please God. I want to be sober. And I'm scared that this might be the last time for me."

"Terri, the bible says that God has a bad memory about the messes we've made. It says He will remember our sins no more. It isn't about what you can do to please Him. It's never been about that. It's about what He wants to do for you. It's about His passionate, crazy love for you. You don't need to do anything to please Him. All you need to do is rest in the knowledge that you are greatly loved by Him."

We arrived at the other hospital and transferred her to the bed. I gave report through the snickers, rolling eyes and giggles of the hospital staff. Before I left the ER, I gave her a big hug and told her I thought she was awesome. I didn't care what they thought about Terri. I really liked her.

Was she healed? I don't know. It's becoming less important to me these days. I do know that she was touched by the love of God and that's what she needed most. When I stand in eternity, looking back at every moment of my life from heaven's perspective, this moment will appear once more before my eyes. I'll know all the results of our meeting down to the smallest detail. Just as it's too late for an alcoholic to go back and change everything after their liver fails, once we step into eternity it will be too late for us to change our actions toward people like Terri.

All we can do is wonder...

What if?

Good Cop—Bad Cop

It was the second day in a row that I worked with an EMT named Randy. He happens to be a Christian and we were getting along pretty well. He was glad to hear that I had been praying with my patients. We talked for a while about how people react when you ask if you can pray with them. I was enjoying a rare moment with someone who sees things the way I do. We were dispatched to pick up someone who needed a ride to the Sobering Center.

We arrived on scene and I introduced Randy and myself to our patient, whose name was Carrie. After we got her loaded in the ambulance, I got her seat belt on and we headed toward the sobering center. Suddenly, Carrie pulled out a lighter and a cigarette. "What are you going to do with those?" I asked.

"What the hell do you think I'm doing with them? I'm gonna have me a smoke."

"No, you're not," I retorted. "We have oxygen onboard. Put 'em away."

"Who the hell are you to tell me where I can smoke? Screw you! I'll smoke wherever I damn well wanna smoke."

"Look Carrie, you're not gonna smoke in my ambulance. Put the lighter and cigarettes away."

"I don't have to listen to you. I guess you don't know this is a free country. I can do whatever the hell I want." She defiantly put the cigarette in her mouth and lit it. Then she took a long drag and blew the smoke in my face.

I stared at her as my anger simmered. Nothing that was going through my mind at the time would help the situation so I said nothing.

She was drunk and belligerent and obviously she wasn't used to following someone else's rules. And a three-minute ride in my ambulance wasn't going to correct a lifetime of habits she'd learned. There was no point in trying to lecture her about manners, but there was no way I was going to let her smoke during the transport. As she put the cigarette to her lips again I quickly grabbed it out of her hand then crushed it up and tossed it on the floor. "Don't try it again."

In cop movies, when two detectives are interrogating a suspect, there's usually one cop who plays the good guy. He questions the suspect but tries to do it in a friendly way. His angle is to get the suspect to cooperate by using diplomacy and kindness. Since suspects don't always cooperate with the good cop, another one will interview the suspect. His demeanor isn't so nice. He would rather just beat the suspect into submission, rather than waste time using diplomacy. The good cop, bad cop dynamic is a staple of Hollywood movies. In EMS, we often run into the same situation. One of us is able to use diplomacy while the other must resort to using force. I prefer to play the good cop, but I got off on the wrong foot with Carrie. I'd already burned my bridges with her so if anything positive was going to come out of this encounter it was up to Randy.

We got her to the Sobering Center without any further hostilities. We helped her out of the ambulance and Randy had a little chat with her. He wanted to leave her with an encouraging word. "You may not know this Carrie, but God has been chasing after you for a long time and one of these days He's gonna catch you. When He does, you're going to realize just how awesome He is and how deeply He loves you." She looked at him in stunned silence.

"Where did that come from?"

"It came from the heart of God, Carrie. He sent me as His messenger to let you know He loves you in spite of all the things you've done."

"He's right, Carrie," I added. "God has given you some amazing gifts. You have the ability to receive revelation in a way that few people do. I'll bet you have some amazing dreams. You may not know this, but God gave you those gifts because He wants you to bless other people with them. He really does love you."

She looked at me and smiled. "There's no way you would know this... but I'm a white witch. I see things in dreams and visions that are gonna happen in the future—all kinds of crazy things. I can see 'em coming in advance." She looked into my eyes. "You're one of them seers, aren't you? I know you are, so don't deny it. You see the future too, don't you?"

"Yeah, I have dreams about future events."

"Ha ha! I knew it!"

Randy put his arm around Carrie's shoulder. "I think it's time we got you inside... we have more calls to run." We walked her inside and found a chair where she could sit down and I introduced her to the woman who would be checking her in. Carrie was a regular client so they were already on a first name basis. I gave her a quick report on what happened during the transport and got her signature. "Do you have any questions?"

"No, I think that covers everything. Thanks for dropping her off."

"Oh, it was definitely our pleasure," I replied.

Randy and I headed for the door. "See you later, Carrie," Randy said as we left. "And remember what I told you. God really does love you."

Morphine or Prayer?

OUR PATIENT TRAVIS HAD BEEN in the hospital for about a week, while doctors ran tests to determine what was causing his chest pain. His EKGs and cardiac enzymes were normal, yet he developed classic cardiac chest pain and shortness of breath with only the slightest exertion. A positive stress test was the only thing so far that pointed to a heart problem.

They finally did a coronary angiogram, which revealed 99% occlusion of one artery and 33% occlusion of two other arteries. The location of the blockage made stent placement risky. They opted for the more traditional approach and scheduled him for 3-vessel bypass surgery. We were the transport crew that would take him to the hospital where the surgery would be done.

Travis had no real medical history. He'd always been healthy. The news of bypass surgery had him a little freaked out. They medicated him for anxiety and pain before we arrived, but he was still scared about the procedure that awaited him.

I was feeling extra bold that morning (maybe it was the coffee) so I told him that my goal was to have him healed before we arrived at the other hospital. He said, "You know... I was praying a lot last night. I really don't want to have this surgery." I asked if I could pray with him, and he gladly agreed.

I wanted to give him hope that he really could be healed, so I shared a few healing testimonies. Each story made him more hopeful. We also needed to treat the chest pain he was having. Although he was on a nitroglycerine drip, which opens up coronary arteries and relieves chest pain, he was still having pain that he rated five on a one to ten scale. A few milligrams of morphine eased the pain a little.

As we drove toward the destination hospital I continued sharing testimonies with him, then asked once more if I could pray with him. He welcomed my prayer with hope.

I placed my hand on his shoulder. "I command Travis's coronary arteries to be healed, opened, and cleared of all occlusions right now. I speak peace and health to his mind and body. Lord Jesus, bring your peace upon him." I asked if he felt any different. My prayers seemed to help as his anxiety decreased the more we talked.

Just before we arrived, his chest pain went back up to five out of ten. I wanted his pain gone, so I gave him a choice between prayer and morphine. He was satisfied to let me pray with him. I placed my hand on his chest. "I command chest pain to leave right now in the name of Jesus. I command arteries to be opened." I asked how bad his pain was.

"It's about a three."

"Chest pain I command you to leave in the name of Jesus. Arteries, be opened right now." I asked again how he felt.

"It's almost gone... maybe a one right now."

After commanding it to leave the third time, all his pain was gone. The look on his face was priceless. I told him it was all about faith and I explained that *my* faith could get him healed, but *his* faith would keep him healed. I told him about the realities of spiritual warfare and that the enemy would probably bring the pain back, trying to convince him he wasn't healed. I told him to continue believing that he was healed, regardless of how he felt. "Resist the enemy and he will flee from you."

Travis was grateful that a stranger introduced him to God's power and love. As I left him in the ICU, he said, "You know, this whole experience really gives me a lot to think about." That's the main point of divine healing. When the kingdom of God lands in your front yard, it's supposed to make you think differently about the issues of life, death, God and eternity.

I'm not sure that his arteries were healed, but I believe they were. Only God knows. And a few minutes after I left the hospital, Travis and his cardiac team would know too. I can just imagine them looking at the arteries that had been occluded 24 hours earlier and wondering what happened.

Burning in Arizona

TEMPE IS HOME TO 70,000 Arizona State University students and one beautiful shopping mall. When we visited Tempe before moving to Arizona, we visited the mall and fell in love with the palm trees, fountains, fireplaces, and friendly people. After we moved into our apartment, we needed lamps so I headed to the mall with my wife and daughter. In one of the stores we met a student and her mother; both decked out in pink from head to toe. Most of the things they bought were also pink. After some playful joking, the daughter warned us not to come shopping there this weekend, because we'd run into tens of thousands of college students buying everything they needed for the school year.

At the end of the evening, while making our way toward the parking lot, we noticed a woman in a wheelchair. I had not yet prayed with anyone since moving here, so I excitedly approached her and started a conversation.

"It's a beautiful day for a little shopping isn't it? I asked as I told her my name.

"Yes, it's a wonderful evening," she replied.

"It's a little warmer than we're accustomed to. We just moved here from Washington and we're not used to the heat yet, but those little things they have on the eves that spray out water are kind of nice."

"Oh, you mean the mist sprayers. Yeah, they do help keep you cool. So what brings you to Tempe?"

"I'm working as a paramedic. My wife got tired of the cold, rainy weather in Washington so I took a job here."

"Well if she likes warm weather you moved to the right place," she said with a chuckle.

The thermometer hit 112 degrees that day and I was dripping with perspiration as we made small talk. Impersonal conversations are the safest kind to engage in when talking with strangers. There's nothing at stake for either party when you talk about the weather, unless one of you happens to be a weather forecaster. I felt like we had become acquainted well enough to move to the next level of conversation, which would be more personal.

"Do you mind if I ask why you're in the wheelchair?"

"I have progressive supranuclear palsy."

"That sounds pretty serious. How would you like to be healed?"

She did a double take and asked, "What did you say?"

I repeated the question, "How would you like to be healed?"

She smiled and asked, "And how are you going to do that?" From her response, I knew she wanted to be healed. If she didn't, she probably would have simply said no, or went on her way.

"Well, I've been praying with my patients for a few years and I see a lot of miracles in my ambulance." I shared some of the stories you've just read and asked if I could pray with her. She said yes.

"Okay, I want you to take my hand." She pulled off a glove from her left hand that she wore to prevent calluses from using the wheelchair. She apologized for a large sore on her hand, explaining that her doctors thought it was cancer but they weren't sure.

"No need to apologize, ma'am. I just want you to be healed." I bent my knees to get down to her level, took her hand and closed my eyes. "Holy Spirit, bring your power and presence upon this daughter of yours. I command her spine, ligaments, nerves, tendons and muscles to be healed. I command all nerves to be healed. I command sickness and spirits of pain to leave in the name of Jesus." When I opened my eyes I noticed she was crying. I asked what she felt.

"Tingling... all over my body... from head to toe." She was deeply touched by God's presence.

"Cool. I think we need a little more of that. Okay Holy Spirit, bring more of your healing presence. I bless your work of healing in her body. I command all sickness and disease to leave right now in the mighty name of Jesus." I asked again what she felt.

"I feel a warm, burning sensation all over. It's not uncomfortable, it feels so nice," she said with a huge smile.

I prayed with her for a few more minutes then told her I believed she was healed. She told me she would love to have her next series of tests show no disease and ask her doctors to explain it. My wife reminded me to tell her how to keep her healing, so we spent a few minutes teaching her about the battle against the enemy. I told her that my faith in God could get her healed, but it was her faith that would keep her healed.

At this point her husband arrived so I introduced my family. He seemed anxious to get her home, so we said goodbye. She didn't try to get out of the wheelchair. But I believe she was healed. We both went home with a better understanding about who God really is.

I think I'm going to like living in Arizona. God is here. He's in me and if you're a Christian, He's in you. All we need to do is let His power and love flow through us.

Training Wreck

MY NEW JOB IN ARIZONA required two long weeks of training and orientation. I survived the first week, which amounted to five days of sitting in a refrigerated classroom fighting off hypothermia, which was mercifully interrupted by short trips to the driving course to run over orange cones in 110-degree heat. I'm not sure what the cones did to deserve this treatment, but fortunately no one was hurt.

The first day of field training was busy and a little bit wild. We were hit by another ambulance in a hospital parking lot and our ambulance ended up on the back of a tow truck. I was given an opportunity to learn how to fill out an incident report and the driver of the other ambulance earned the privilege of going back to driving school to run over more orange cones. The second day my ventilator broke. I just wanted to survive the rest of my training rides without any major problems.

Today, my training instructor called out sick before the shift began, so I was supervised by someone who doesn't normally do training. He was a nice guy who really helped me understand the system and he had some great tips to help me be successful. Our EMT for the day was a quiet young man, who looked barely old enough to vote. I know he's had some problems making the adjustment here. Between calls we talked a little and I learned that he's hoping to get hired by one of the local fire departments.

We were in an older back-up ambulance that had a few mechanical issues—the major one being a weak air conditioner. In the heat of the afternoon I felt like a quart of ice cream sitting in the sun. My wife sent me a text message asking if she could meet us somewhere for dinner.

I told her that would be nice but I had no idea where we were. For the last three days I've been looking at the hills and freeways of Phoenix through the back window of an ambulance. Our EMT has driven us from one end of this cactus-covered valley to the other. Every time we stopped, I had to ask where we were. I'd never been so lost in my life.

The other thing about our ambulance is that it has a rear bumper that sticks out a little farther than most ambulances. Our EMT rammed his knee into the bumper halfway through the shift and spent the rest of the day limping. So at the end of the day, without much explanation, I told the guys that if they ever had an injury, to come see me before they had surgery. Our EMT said, "Hey, what about my knee? It still hurts a lot."

I jokingly replied, "Dude... it's just a soft tissue injury. Walk it off."

I've been uneasy about praying with people at my new job. I don't want to cause problems or have people complain. But I really hate seeing injured people suffer needlessly. When we got back to the station at the end of the day we had to make several trips to unload equipment. On one of the trips, the injured EMT and I ended up at the back of the ambulance at the same time. I told him to sit on the bench seat and I asked the usual questions—how bad was the pain, where exactly did it hurt, etc.

I placed two fingers on his knee and said, "I command ligaments, tendons, bones, muscles, nerves and soft tissue to be healed in Jesus' name. Holy Spirit, bring your power and presence. I command the spirit of pain to leave in Jesus' name. Well... how does it feel?"

He stood up and immediately realized all the pain was gone. He looked at me with a smile of wonderment and jumped out the back door of the ambulance. His happiness got the best of him as he walked around, dumbfounded that his knee was instantly healed. I got out of the ambulance and he gave me a high five. "Go ahead, I said. "Test it out as much as you want. You're not going to wreck what God healed."

I'm in training for a lot of things right now. Some of my training helps me learn how to work in a new EMS system. But another part of my training is learning to reign with Jesus in His kingdom. If you're a believer, you're training to reign too.

My Head is Tingling

IN THE EYES OF MOST paramedics, there is little glory in transferring depressed, intoxicated patients from one hospital to another for mental health evaluations. These aren't the calls we tell our friends about when we get together, unless it's to make derogatory comments. Shania had been in Phoenix just long enough to develop a nice suntan. Like me, she'd moved here a month ago. She lost her job and her boyfriend and having no other support system, she moved in with a friend. But her old pals—depression and suicidal thoughts—moved with her, and they were making her life a living hell. After 24 hours of torment in the emergency department, we showed up to take her to a different hospital. After I introduced my partner and myself and got report from her nurse, we loaded her in the back of the ambulance.

I got the formal questions out of the way and had most of my charting done after a few minutes. I wanted to spend most of the trip learning about her problems and perhaps getting the Holy Spirit involved. After learning we were both new to Phoenix, she told me she was from San Jose, which made me think about my friends from the bay area who do street healing. I told her about how they go to shopping malls and occasionally emergency rooms to heal people. She wanted to hear more about them.

I shared some history of the healing movement in northern California then about ten minutes of my own stories. Her curiosity grew and she thought about her mother who had a lot of medical problems, who lived in San Jose. She asked for contact information for some of my friends in the Bay area. I wrote their info on the back of my website card for her mom and told her she could e-mail or find me on Facebook if she had any questions.

I asked if she had any pain. She said she had fibromyalgia. I asked if her symptoms began after an emotionally traumatic event. "Yeah, I was in a very abusive relationship and right after it ended, I began having pain."

I believe (although I'm not dogmatic about it) that fibromyalgia is a manifestation of a spirit that attacks people after emotionally traumatic events. I asked if I could pray with her. She smiled and said, "Sure."

I placed my hand on her shoulder. "Holy Spirit bring your presence into the ambulance and touch Shania with your power. Bring healing of her memories and remove the thoughts that torment her. Spirit of trauma I command you to leave now in the name of Jesus. Pain and inflammation get out!" I asked if she felt anything.

"My head is tingling."

"Do you feel tingling anywhere else?"

"Nope. It's just my head."

I looked again at her and noticed she was crying tears of joy. She knew that God was touching her. "Shania, I believe the tingling is God's way of healing your mind, emotions, and memories."

Some of you might be wondering... why tingling?

I'm happy to answer that question.

All our senses: sight, sound, smell, taste and touch (including pain) travel along nerves in our body. The nervous system is like a bundle of electrical wires, carrying impulses through millions of cells strung end to end.

When the power of God goes through a part of our body, wouldn't we expect our own electrical system to be affected by it and send signals to our brain letting us know something was happening? I believe this is why so many people feel tingling when God is healing them.

We were almost at the destination, so I spent the rest of the trip teaching her about the battle to keep her healing. "If the symptoms leave, they might return. But if they do, don't freak out. It's just the enemy trying to convince you that you weren't healed. Just stand by faith and believe God has healed you and if you feel like you need to command the symptoms to leave, go ahead and do it." We arrived and unloaded the gurney and wheeled her inside.

"I just want to thank you for caring about me. What would I do if God didn't send people like you in your ambulance to help people like me?"

She gave me a hug and I gave her another one of my website cards to keep for herself. "Shania, here's my e-mail address. If you have any problems, drop me a line."

Was she healed? I don't know. But I do know she was touched by God and that's what matters most. I introduce them to God, and the Holy Spirit takes it from there.

I didn't see those two old men "depression" and "suicide" during the transport. They come in through open doors. Like uninvited guests, they see an opening and come around to harass defenseless people. They enter because there is no door to keep them out—just a big hole in our life that leaves us vulnerable to attack from the enemy. Jesus said, "I am the door."

When The Door shows up, that hole in your life can be closed off to intruders like fear, depression, worry, anxiety, guilt and shame. Jesus is our only defense against them. Shania knows that Jesus is real and that He cares about her. Maybe she'll learn that He's her door of safety, too.

Most medics don't see the glory in psychiatric transfers because they're looking for something that glorifies them. If you want to be a hero, you need to show off your skills. Healing doesn't require skill and it doesn't bring glory to us. It brings glory to God and it's not our skill, but His power on display. Some people don't like others being in the spotlight. But I'm cool with it. My only hope of glory is that Christ will be formed in me.

Among Friends

ONE PROBLEM WITH MOVING TO a new area is finding a good hair stylist. I don't have that problem, thanks to some weird genes I got from my dad. But my wife likes to look her best and I appreciate that. She has a philosophy about finding a stylist that works for her. When she sees a woman with nice looking hair, she asks what salon she goes to. Last night was her first appointment at a salon called *Among Friends*.

With all the crazy Holy Spirit fun we had with her last hair stylist, I had high hopes for her new one.

Would she be a Christian?

Would she need healing?

Would she have a sense of humor?

Or would she think we were crazy?

After we arrived at the salon, I walked with my daughter across the street to get a Slurpee while Mary and my wife got acquainted. When we got back to the salon, it didn't take long before our questions were answered. We talked about what brought us to Arizona and some of the things we'd done since the move. I wanted to know if she attended church, so I mentioned that we visited a church in Tucson that had some cool ministries. She responded with a lot of information on the local church and Christian music scene. Chris Tomlin is one of her favorite singers, which gave me an immediate connection, since he's one of the people who inspired me to start playing guitar.

I told her about some of the amazing things God had done with us recently, mostly about dreams and healing. She was fascinated. As she clipped and styled my wife's hair, I shared some of the more unusual healing testimonies. My wife had a job interview the following day. Mary said, "I know you'll get the job. Everyone who comes to me before a job interview gets the job they interview for. It's like my ministry to people. I give them hairstyles for success."

A young boy came to the door and Mary went to see what he wanted. As she walked, my daughter noticed her limping slightly and mentioned it to me. I looked and sure enough, I could see either her right hip or right knee was giving her problems. When she returned, I asked what happened to make her limp. Slightly embarrassed, she pulled up her pant leg revealing some scabbed-over puncture wounds. Looking closer at her knee, I could see it was swollen. She explained, "I tripped and fell on some rocks. My knee has been in a lot of pain ever since."

"Well then, why don't we get you healed before we leave?"

As Mary put a few finishing touches on my wife's hair, we continued talking about God and the great things He had done for us. She kept saying she was part of our family. Mary has a strong love for the people of God. The hour we spent with her was like a long-awaited family reunion. When the hair styling was done, we had her sit in the chair. I gave her a short lesson on healing.

"Mary, if you read Luke, Chapter 10, you'll find that Jesus gave His disciples a commission to heal the sick, raise the dead, cast out demons and proclaim the kingdom of God. When Peter and John found the crippled man who begged for money at the gate called "Beautiful," Peter said to him, 'Silver and gold I do not have, but what I do have I give you: In the name of Jesus Christ of Nazareth, rise up and walk.' They took his hand and stood him up and he was healed. We're disciples of Jesus and we do the same thing. So on a scale from one to ten how bad is your pain?"

"It's about an eight."

I had my daughter lay hands on her and pray. She immediately felt something moving in her knee and a slightly cool sensation. My wife and I joined in. "I command ligaments, tendons, cartilage, nerves and bones to be healed in the name of Jesus." My wife prayed in tongues. I asked Mary what she felt.

Not surprisingly, she said, "tingling." We had her stand up. She was able to walk with only slight pain. I asked if we could pray one more time, so she sat down and we prayed again. She got up from the chair amazed and walked around the salon without any pain.

The hair appointment turned into a hug fest. Before leaving, we prayed for her to have dreams from God, since she hasn't had any in years. We hated the fact that we had to leave, but it was getting late and I had to get up early for work the next day. So that was our adventure at the hair salon. God is so in love with people. He loves to demonstrate his love through people like you and me.

※

Mary continues to be my wife's hair stylist. Years later, I'm happy to report that she still talks about that day when God miraculously healed her knee. She never had any return of symptoms or pain.

When Seeing is Believing

AFTER MOVING TO PHOENIX I worked with a different partner every day for a while. One day my latest partner and I transported a woman named Cecilia who complained of numbness in her right leg from her groin to her toes. Her doctor ordered an ultrasound, suspecting she had an injury to one of the blood vessels in her leg. A few weeks earlier she'd had a heart attack and as a result, had a stent place in one of her coronary arteries to keep it open. To insert a stent, they place a large needle into a blood vessel in the groin and advance it to the heart. Our suspicion was that the insertion site for the catheter in her groin might have developed an aneurysm, compressing the femoral nerve, causing numbness to her leg.

To complicate the picture, Cecilia had kidney failure and was on dialysis. The dialysis fistula in her left arm deteriorated to the point where it was no longer useful. So her surgeon tied it off and following the surgery, she developed pain and some loss of function in her left hand. She also had complete blindness in her left eye and partial blindness in her right eye from detached retinas. The facility she lived at was across the parking lot from the hospital. No pressure on me at all. I had a few hundred feet of blacktop in which to work a miracle.

As we wheeled Cecilia toward the elevator, I asked if she'd let me pray for her to be healed. She agreed, so I started with her left hand. She reported the severity of pain as six out of ten. As the elevator door opened, I went to work. I placed my hand on her forearm. "I commanded pain to leave right now in the name of Jesus." After the door closed, I asked how she felt.

"I don't feel anything, now."

"Do you feel any pain in your arm or hand?"

Smiling, and flexing her wrist and fingers in amazement, she said, "No pain at all. It feels normal."

The elevator door opened and we wheeled her toward the ambulance and loaded the gurney. I needed to get a set of vital signs and some more information then call the receiving hospital. I asked my partner to get in back of the ambulance for a few minutes. I didn't actually need her help. I just wanted her to see what was about to happen. I did a brief neurological assessment of Cecilia's right leg. She felt nothing when I ran my finger along the sole of her foot. I did it several times to make sure. Next I pinched her skin above her ankle.

"I can feel you touching me, but I can't tell if it's dull or sharp," she said.

Just below her knee, she could tell I was pinching her skin. The neurologic deficit was slight at the knee, progressively getting worse toward the foot, which had no sensation at all. I placed my hand on her leg. "Holy Spirit touch Cecilia with your presence. I command nerves and blood vessels to be healed in the name of Jesus." I asked if she felt anything.

With a smile she replied, "My whole leg is tingling."

I rubbed the bottom of her foot again and asked if she felt anything. "Yes, I can feel you touching the bottom of my foot." I pinched the skin above her ankle. "I can feel you pinching me." All the numbness in her leg was now gone.

My partner looked on in quiet amazement. Finally breaking her silence she said, "I think you may have just made a believer out of me."

I turned to her and said, "This is the kind of healing Jesus did when He walked the streets of Galilee. He healed the sick, gave sight to the blind and opened the ears of the deaf. And He gave his disciples authority to do the same things."

Finally, I began praying for her eyes. Each time I commanded her eyes to see, she reported more light coming into her right eye, but no improvement in her left eye. Not every healing is instant; some healing takes a little more time. I made the call to the hospital, but continued praying over her eyes until we arrived.

We transferred her to the ER and I gave report. When the nurse left the room, I thanked Cecilia for letting me pray with her. "I'm glad you're being healed Cecilia, and I believe you will eventually see normally out of both eyes." This was important for my new partner. She'd never seen a miracle of healing and it probably changed her beliefs about God. After we left the hospital we found a shady spot to park and waited for the next call. We talked about healing and God. I shared some testimonies and she let me pray for her back to be healed.

Someone once said, "Preach the gospel at all times. Use words if necessary." Today, my partner (a complete stranger no less) saw the gospel in action. I never said a word to her about God until after our patient was healed. No preaching was needed. We didn't talk about creation or evolution or sin. A simple miracle of healing compelled her to confess a change of heart.

For some of us, seeing is believing. If that's true, perhaps we should let the world see more of our Jesus in action.

Show & Tell

WE MADE A LOT OF trips to the hardware store after we moved into our new home. On this particular trip we needed a special light bulb for my daughter's new lamp, a bolt and a couple of nuts for one of our beds. We hadn't been in the store for two minutes when I saw a woman approaching us. She was riding in an electric cart for people with disabilities. I noticed she had an immobilizer on her left foot. I walked up to her, asked her name and introduced myself. "Do you mind if I ask what happened to your foot?"

"I sprained my ankle pretty bad," she replied. "I'm going to see my doctor when I leave here." Her teenaged son was with her. I turned to him.

"Do you know that Jesus went around healing all kinds of people in public?"

"I learned about that in Sunday school," he replied.

"So you know He went around Israel healing the sick, giving sight to the blind and casting out demons, but did you know He gave his disciples the authority to do it too?"

"He did?"

"He sure did. Have you ever seen a miracle?" I asked. He shook his head no. "Healing the sick is something any believer can do and I believe your mom's foot is going to be healed. Ma'am, would you mind if I prayed for your foot to be healed?"

"I wouldn't mind at all."

I placed my hand on her foot and had her son stand where he could see what I was doing. "Holy Spirit bring your power and presence and touch this dear woman. Pain and inflammation leave. Spirits of pain I command you to leave. Ligaments and tendons be healed in the name of Jesus." I explained to her son everything I did as he looked on with interest.

"Ma'am, are you feeling anything different in your foot?"

"It feels hot on the side of my foot."

I placed my hand on her foot again. Speaking to her son I said, "Okay, now watch what I'm doing because one day you're going to be doing this. All I do is place my hand near the injury and command it to be healed. It's really that simple most of the time. Ligaments, muscles, tendons and cartilage, I command you to be healed." I asked what she felt.

"The heat is higher up in my leg now."

"Is there any pain?"

"A little."

I placed my hand on the immobilizer one more time. "Spirit of pain, get out now. Inflammation leave." I asked again how she felt.

She wiggled her foot around. "Seems like it's pretty much gone."

"I've always wanted to do this," I said with a childish grin. Can I remove the immobilizer and have you walk around to see if it's healed?" She agreed, so I unfastened the Velcro straps and took the immobilizer off. She stood up and walked around in front of me.

"There's a little pressure on the side of my foot, but the pain is gone," she said smiling.

I gave her some instruction on how to keep her healing and encouraged her son to consider learning more about it. I gave them a card to my website and told her to contact me if she had any questions or wanted to share her testimony.

It's a show and tell gospel. We give people information about God. Demonstrate His love for them and show it by displaying His power. It's not complicated. It's actually pretty simple.

One light bulb—$3.59

One bolt and two nuts—$.32

Releasing the power of God and discipling his children—priceless.

When Wells Fargo Tells You to Pray

MOVING FROM WASHINGTON TO ARIZONA was a big step of faith. Our move to the Phoenix area wasn't something God actually called us to do. From the beginning, we realized it was completely our decision to move. The weather, lower housing prices and several other factors made it a desirable location for us. Most of you know we're strongly led in our walk with God by our dreams. Prior to moving, I didn't have a single dream about Arizona, except one dream we had three weeks before moving. One morning I woke up from a dream and as usual, I wrote it down on an index card so I wouldn't forget it. A few minutes later my wife woke up. I said to her, "I had an interesting dream honey."

"So did I," she replied.

I gave her a kiss. "Why don't you tell me yours first?"

She said, "Well, I was in this office. I think it was a title company. I was sitting at a desk signing papers to close on a home loan."

I looked at her and began giggling. "You're not going to believe this. I had the same dream!"

"What do you mean the same dream?"

In my dream I was in an office signing papers to close on a home loan.

"Are you serious?" She asked.

"Dead serious. You know... I've always wanted us to have the same dream on the same night. Never thought it would actually happen."

When we moved, we decided to do a short-term (month to month) lease on an apartment. We didn't want to commit to a one-year lease on a small apartment, believing we would find a home to buy quickly. Sure enough, within two weeks of moving, we found the house we wanted. We made an offer and it was accepted. We began making plans to move and started getting things in order for the home loan.

Going into the process of getting the loan we had some problems to overcome. I took a fifty percent cut in pay when I moved to Phoenix and my wife was interviewing but hadn't found a job yet. We had to qualify on my income alone and that meant I had to work a lot of overtime to show the bank we could afford the loan.

We also ran into a problem over my hourly pay. My employer agreed to an hourly wage if I could prove I'd never had a lapse in my paramedic license going all the way back to 1988. It took several weeks and a lot of phone calls to various agencies in different states, but I got what they wanted. Unfortunately, my employer decided not to honor the agreement. They started me at the bottom of the pay scale and the raise they ultimately decided to give me was less than what we agreed to.

The week before the bank was going to look at my paycheck to see if my income was enough to qualify for the loan I still had not received the raise my employer promised. We knew if the company didn't change my wage immediately, we wouldn't qualify.

So, after I got off duty that Friday, I made a call to the human resource department at work. Unfortunately, it was 4:30 p.m. and their office was about to close for the week. Nothing like last minute details! I had only 30 minutes to get through to find out what was going on with my raise. When I called, I kept having problems getting through to a real person. I even got disconnected a few times, sending my wife into near panic. When my call finally did get transferred to a real person, it wasn't the right person and they would have to transfer me again. Time was running short. This craziness went on until one employee finally sensed our urgency, left her desk, and walked through the building looking for someone who could help me.

The answer was not what we wanted. She told me my raise had not been approved by the general manager because he was in the hospital. Payroll went out Monday morning. The change had to be approved by then or our window of opportunity would be gone.

We prayed. Actually, we had been praying a lot even prior to this because we went through almost daily setbacks in this loan process. My prayer was basically a declaration. In my heart, I felt the dream God gave us was a promise that we'd get the house. A few of our friends were in on the drama and they prayed with us. You have no idea how important it was for us to know someone was standing with us.

The Supernatural Journal of a Former Atheist Paramedic

I knew there was no one in the company working over the weekend that could approve my raise. It simply couldn't happen. But on Monday morning, I still needed to see if God had worked some sort of miracle over the weekend. I logged on to the company website out of curiosity to check on my hourly pay rate. Much to my surprise, my raise went through over the weekend! I was so surprised that I drove to the human resource office to talk to someone about it. I met with the same woman I had spoken with on Friday afternoon. "Hi, I spoke with you on Friday about my raise."

"Oh yes, I remember you."

"I logged on to the company website this morning out of curiosity to see if my raise went through. I was really surprised to see that it was approved. I almost can't believe it's true. Would you check?"

"Really? That's odd. I was under the impression it wouldn't be approved since the division general manager has to approve it and he's been in the hospital. Let me take a look." She logged onto the website and checked on my pay. "Well it seems you're right. The system shows that your raise was approved sometime Friday afternoon."

"But when I spoke to you on Friday afternoon you said there's no way it could be approved until after the weekend."

"Yes, I remember saying that."

"I don't mean to sound ungrateful. I'm happy the raise was approved, but if the general manager was in the hospital and he couldn't approve my raise, who did?"

"I have no idea."

"Thank you. I guess we'll be going now." I began to wonder if maybe God sent an angel into the manager's office to approve my raise. Yay God! But we're not out of the woods yet.

The home inspection was done and not surprisingly, we had some small repairs to take care of. There were small cracks in the joints between the tiles on the roof, which could potentially cause water damage if they were not repaired. The side yard gate needed repair and a few other minor things showed up on the report. The inspector was certain the loan would not go through until the repair to the roof had been made. We expected to hear from the owner about how we'd get the repairs done before closing, but the call never came.

Then we got a call from our loan officer who informed us that underwriting was requiring no repairs before closing. We were shocked. So was the loan officer. "I've been doing loans a long time and this is the first time I've ever seen this happen. They always find something that needs to be fixed. I don't get it." So he double-checked with underwriting and sure enough—we could close without making any repairs. This is how the entire process went. One potential obstacle followed by an unexpected and hard to believe solution that miraculously materialized.

But we had other problems in underwriting. They were looking at my income and they kept finding problems. My wife wrote off a business loss from the prior year and they wanted an explanation. Then it turned out that my income, because it contained a lot of overtime, was in question. They contacted my employer a number of times to verify the facts and every time they did, my employer told them something that made things even worse.

One Friday afternoon, our loan officer called and gave my wife more bad news. "Hi guys. How are you doing? It's been a pretty hectic week with underwriting. I was wondering if you guys believe in prayer."

My wife replied, "We've been praying ever since we made the offer. What's going on?"

"You'll probably want to keep praying this weekend. You're going to need some help if the loan is going to go through. We don't have a clear-cut answer from underwriting yet. It looks like you've got a borderline case—it could go either way. It's completely up to the discretion of the underwriter."

I'll admit we were concerned at times. But every time worry reared its head, we thought about the dreams and about all the things God had already done for us. He made a promise and we just knew He'd keep it.

On Friday, the loan officer would call with bad news. We'd pray and make declarations over the weekend. On Monday or Tuesday, he would call with good news. That's how it went almost every week. In spite of the uncertainties, we gave notice that we were moving out of the apartment and scheduled movers to help us, though we didn't have a firm approval or a closing date yet on the home loan. One day my wife received another call from the bank.

"Guys, we're coming down to the wire regarding your deposit money. There's a point in this process before which if you withdraw your offer, or if you don't qualify for the loan, we can refund your deposit. The time is fast approaching where you're going to lose your deposit money if the loan doesn't go through. You have to make a choice. You either need to keep your offer on the table and hope you're approved, at the risk of losing your deposit, or you can withdraw your offer."

We discussed the option of withdrawing our offer, but at this point we were both convinced that God was going to make it happen. My wife explained to our loan officer, "We both had a dream on the same night that we were in an office signing papers to close on the loan. We're taking it as a promise from God that the loan will be approved, so we're keeping our offer on the table."

It was a good move as we were eventually approved for the loan. We had put down a cash deposit, but our closing money was invested in silver bullion. At some point we had to cash it out and deposit the money in escrow for closing. A few days before closing, we cashed out the silver. On the day we cashed it out, the spot price for silver was a little over $40 an ounce. Three days later, the spot price had dropped to $28 an ounce. God allowed us to cash out our silver at the perfect time, just before the price dropped.

It was September 29th; the day before we were supposed to close on the loan, but the bank had not yet given us an official closing date. We had to be out of our apartment tomorrow and have our storage units empty if we didn't want to pay for another month. On the morning of the 30th (the day of our scheduled move) the loan officer called and said, "We're going to try to close late in the morning today."

We scheduled the movers to pick up our stuff that morning but now we wouldn't be able to help them because we had to go to the title company to sign the papers for closing. We had our teenaged daughter help the movers and we got the manager to open the storage units and told the movers we'd meet up with them in a few hours at the house after we signed the papers. Hopefully, we'd have the keys to the house.

It turned out we didn't get the keys. The seller of the house didn't show up at signing and our realtor wasn't able to contact them. Nobody knew where the keys were. So we had movers on the clock and they were just about ready to drop off our stuff but we couldn't get in the house. Well, what the heck... it's not like we didn't anticipate something like this was going to happen.

I had the movers begin to unload our furniture in the driveway. Calls were made and our realtor finally asked us to check inside the breaker panel outside the house. We looked and sure enough, we found a key hidden inside the breaker panel.

The process of moving and buying the house was one of the most stressful and yet, one of the most splendidly divine ordeals I've ever been through. The hand of God was all over this thing. And the crowning jewel came about a week later when we received a call from our loan officer. "I want to congratulate you two on pulling off one of the craziest home purchases I've ever witnessed. I also want to apologize for how the closing was delayed. We really dropped the ball on this one. I feel terrible about all the trouble we put you through. The bank wants to show its appreciation for your business so they've authorized me to make a donation on behalf of the bank, in the amount equal to one month's mortgage to the charity of your choice in your name so you'll receive the tax deduction for the donation. So, we'll need the payment information and address for the charity you'd like to choose."

We were speechless. Who ever heard of a bank making a donation to a charity because they made a mistake? We gave him the name of a ministry run by a friend. It operates on a shoestring budget. I called the guy in charge of the ministry and gave him the news. "Now I need some information from you so the bank can make the donation." He was elated by the news, but he had some news of his own to share.

"You're not going to believe this," he said.

"Try me."

"Yesterday I was praying, and for some reason I asked God to send someone from Arizona to help finance something He had put on my heart. I wasn't even sure I knew anyone in Arizona. Today you called with the answer to my prayer."

⌒

The ministry received the donation from Wells Fargo Bank and we had a nice tax deduction that year, courtesy of the Chief Financial Officer of heaven. In the midst of our loan process, we would have rather had smooth sailing than all that turmoil. But looking back, we're grateful God had the bigger picture.

"For My thoughts are not your thoughts, nor are your ways My ways," says the Lord. "For as the heavens are higher than the earth, so are My ways higher than your ways, And My thoughts than your thoughts. (Isaiah 55:8-9)

Watch One, Do One, Teach One

dis·ci·ple
noun
1. a learner, pupil, follower of a school of thought

THERE'S AN OLD SAYING IN emergency medicine: "Watch one, do one, teach one." The idea is that most of the tasks we do aren't complicated. After watching something being demonstrated, we should be able to do it ourselves. After doing it once or twice, we should be able to teach someone else to do it. That, in a nutshell, is how you make a disciple.

I transported a precious little girl, who was about a month old. Nothing serious was going on with her. But during the transport I got into a conversation with her mom, who told me she'd been praying for a few things. One thing led to another and pretty soon we had a church meeting in the back of the ambulance.

Tina told me she was a nursing student and we talked about working in health care and how it opens doors to people who need prayer. I told her some of my stories and the next thing you know she asked how I got people healed. Demonstrating is usually the best way to teach so I asked her to extend her left arm so I could pretend I was healing her. She said, "It's kinda funny that you're doing this, because I actually need healing of that wrist."

"You do?"

"Yeah. I have carpal tunnel syndrome and it kinda hurts right now."

"Cool. Well, I mean… it's not cool that you have carpal tunnel, but it's cool that I can get you healed and show you how it's done at the same time."

She kept her arm extended as I explained the process. I always invite the Holy Spirit to bring his presence and touch people." She seemed to get that part pretty easily. "The next thing I usually do is close my eyes to see if the Holy Spirit wants to show me anything. Sometimes I'll see spirits and when I do, I tell them to get lost. Next I command pain and inflammation to leave and for ligaments, nerves, tendons, muscles and bones to be healed."

"Seems pretty simple," she said.

"Yeah, I try to keep it simple. So are you ready?"

"I sure am!" She said.

I placed my hand on her wrist. "Okay Holy Spirit, bring your presence and touch Tina. Carpal tunnel, I command you to open. Ligaments and tendons be healed right now in the name of Jesus." I asked what she felt.

"It feels warm."

I asked if it still hurt. She flexed her wrist. "Yeah, it still hurts a little."

"If there is any pain after the first time you pray, it's a good idea to pray a second or third or even a fourth time because some healing takes a bit longer. If the person allows me to keep at it, I just keep praying as long as it takes to get them pain-free." I prayed again and she continued feeling heat as the pain gradually subsided. With the enthusiasm she had for healing and after witnessing her own healing, I wouldn't be surprised if she finds herself teaching others how to heal the sick.

Watch one.

Do one.

Teach one.

That's how we make disciples.

My Partner Was a Door Gunner

NOT ALL EMERGENCY MEDICAL TECHNICIANS discover their calling straight out of high school. Some of us work strange jobs on the way to becoming an EMT. The guy I worked with today took some interesting detours. My normal partner was gone for a while on another assignment. My temporary partner called out sick. So today I worked with a guy who doesn't have a regular partner or unit.

As twilight approached and I loaded the gear in my ambulance, six o'clock was drawing near and so was my partner. Ken had been an aircraft mechanic for years and loved being around anything with wings or rotors. In the past, he worked on helicopters for the army. He also spent time on the trigger of an M-60 as a door gunner over Iraq.

We called dispatch to let them know we were ready for the start of our shift and they gave us an assignment to cover an area on the west side of Phoenix. We both needed coffee so when we got there we found a gas station. We called dispatch to let them know we arrived at our destination and they immediately moved us to a different location. Back on the road, we chatted about jobs, friends, good times, marriage ups and downs, kids, and the painful memories that come with the kind of work we do. He told me that the last time he was deployed, his wife didn't object to him going overseas. He thought it was odd, but he didn't ask why. A few days after he got to Afghanistan, she filed for divorce. He's been driving back and forth to court hearings in LA and he doesn't have a penny to his name right now.

After chatting with a buddy who deployed with him to Afghanistan (whose life was saved by Ken's quick thinking) he decided he might do well in EMT school, so he sign up and completed his training. This was his first job in EMS. He'd been with the firm for two months, just like me. He had no idea he was going to have an encounter with God in less than an hour.

We found a spot that would provide shade during the heat of the day and Wi-Fi access for my laptop. Bloggers need to stay connected to the mother ship and I had some serious writing planned for today, if time allowed. We make our plans and God makes His. A few minutes later we got a call to downtown Phoenix. Traffic was picking up and the freeway was a parking lot so we took side roads to get to the call. On the way he told me about this pain in the middle of his back.

Stop me if you've heard this one before.

"How long have you had the pain?"

"A couple of days. I think I strained a muscle."

"On a one to ten scale how bad is it?"

"About a five."

I told him a few stories about people I had seen healed before we arrived on scene. The call was for a non-emergency transfer of a patient going from one hospital to another. We had a few minutes to spare so before we unloaded the gurney I asked, "Do you want to be healed?"

He looked at me a little surprised, but said, "Sure".

"Are you absolutely sure?"

"Yeah, I'm sure," he said with a smile.

"Okay, why don't we get you healed before we go inside? Turn around for a second."

He turned to face away from me and I placed my hand on the middle of his back. "Holy Spirit, bring your presence and power. Pain I command you to leave right now in Jesus' name. Muscles be healed." I asked what he felt.

"That's crazy." He said. "I feel tingling all over my back!"

"That's the power of God healing you." I repeated the process and asked what he felt.

"Wow. This is really crazy. It feels pretty good now."

"Is there any pain at all?"

"Yeah, there's still a little tightness."

I repeated the process one more time and asked what he felt. He twisted as far as he could to the left then right, bent backward and forward trying to see if he could make the pain come back. "There isn't any pain at all! Man... this is crazy!"

We went inside and transported our patient, who had a hole in her heart. She was going from one hospital to another for surgery to close up the hole. She was nice, but rather large. At 348 pounds, we should have called for a bariatric gurney and another crew for lifting help. But my partner was up to the challenge having just been healed by God.

He spent the rest of the morning twisting from side to side every time we stopped. Every time he checked, there still wasn't any pain and he exclaimed, "Man... this is crazy!" We talked about God. I told him about Jesus and the Holy Spirit. The cool thing about divine healing is that it allows God to be the topic of conversation for as long as you want. But my partner had another problem that needed the attention of Doctor Jesus.

During his time overseas he'd had close calls with a mortar explosion and an IED (improvised explosive device) that gave him a few scars. Eventually, he left the army and began working as a civilian contractor. He said he would have gone back in the army if he hadn't partially torn his Achilles tendon, which made it hard for him to run. The VA wanted to do surgery to try to repair it, but he decided to live with it the way it was. I told him, "God is going to heal you before the end of our shift."

Just before the end of shift, dispatch assigned us to post at a hospital. I told him to get out of the ambulance. It was time to be healed. We walked to the back of the ambulance and I had him put his injured foot on the rear bumper. "Is there any pain in your Achilles tendon right now?"

"Not right now. It doesn't hurt unless I run." I had him flex his foot as far as he could. "Okay, that hurts," he said.

"Watch carefully what I'm going to do, because one day you're going to be doing this for other people." I placed my hand near his heel. "Holy Spirit, bring your presence. Tendon, I command you to reattach to the heel bone right now in Jesus' name." I waited a few seconds then asked what he felt.

"This is crazy. I feel like it's swelling up. Like when your foot goes to sleep and then it kinda throbs... that's what it feels like."

"That's God healing you. Flex it again and tell me if it hurts."

He flexed his foot. "Yeah, it still hurts a little."

I placed my hand on the back of his foot. "Lord, bring more of your power. Tendon I command you to reattach right now. Spirit of pain I command you to leave. Inflammation leave now." I asked again what he felt.

"Wow. This is just crazy."

"Dude, that's the kingdom of God," I replied with a smile.

We got in the ambulance and finished out our shift.

༄

A few months later I happened to run into Ken at work and we talked about how he was doing. The back pain never returned. I asked about his Achilles tendon. He said he did some hiking on Camelback Mountain after we prayed and he had no pain or problems with it. He was still amazed at the healing and he was telling his partners about his miracle.

A Second Chance

AMY SAT A FEW FEET away from me during our new employee orientation class. When we had to tell the group what we did, she said she was a detail technician. I didn't even know we hired detail techs. Her job was to clean up after us. When we cover the ambulance in mud, she washes it. When we leave fast food garbage on the floor, she cleans it up. My mother doesn't work here, but Amy does and I'm glad we have people like her in the company.

Early one morning as she made her way out to the wash bay, I noticed that she was limping and asked what was wrong. She showed me her painful, swollen knee, wrapped in a support device. I asked if I could pray with her to be healed. With some fear about what I planned to do, she agreed. When I placed my hand on her knee, she nervously asked, "What are you going to do?"

Removing my hand, I said, "I'm going to pray, is that alright?"

"Yeah that's fine," She replied with a bit of reluctance in her voice.

I place my hand on her knee again. "You're not going to hurt me are you?" She asked.

Removing my hand I replied, "No, why on earth would I hurt you?"

I placed my hand on her knee again. "Spirit of pain I command you to leave in the name of Jesus. Inflammation go. Ligaments, tendons, cartilage, bones and muscles be healed in the name of Jesus." I asked if she felt any different.

"No. It feels the same."

I prayed over her knee two more times but she felt nothing. On the same day that I prayed with Amy, I prayed with the EMT from the previous story that had a partially torn Achilles tendon and back pain. He was healed, but she wasn't. That day and for a few days following, I asked God why one person was healed and the other wasn't. Here's what I heard:

The man with the Achilles tendon injury was healed because he gladly received his healing without fear or worry. Amy was afraid I would hurt her and her fear prevented her from being healed. It wasn't that God could not heal her. It wasn't that He didn't want her healed. It was because she could not receive healing in a state of fear.

I was disappointed. I really wanted her to be healed. I'd seen her a few times since then still walking with a limp. A few months later she saw me loading my gear in the ambulance. She came over and stood beside me.

"I've wanted to ask you a question. When you prayed for me, why wasn't I healed?"

"That's a good question. The day that I prayed with you, I prayed with someone else who was healed. That night I asked God why he was healed and you weren't."

"What did He tell you?"

"He said it was because you were afraid of being hurt. Why did you think I was going to hurt you?"

"My father asked me the same question you did: 'Do you want to be healed?' When I said 'yes,' he hit me hard on my injured knee. So when you asked, I was afraid you would do the same thing."

"I have no reason to hurt you, and if you want to be healed, the offer is still open. God will heal you."

"I want to be healed," she replied hopefully.

"Well then let's have a seat and get this done." We sat on the couch in the day room at our station. She rolled up her pant leg and showed me her swollen knee, wrapped in a black elastic bandage. I placed my hand on her knee.

I wanted her to feel God's presence first, so I started by asking, "Lord, bring your presence upon Amy," and asked what she felt.

"I feel really relaxed and at peace."

"I love it when He does that," I said with a smile. "Being relaxed and free of distraction is always good when receiving healing. I command swelling, inflammation and pain to leave right now in the name of Jesus. Ligaments, tendons, muscles, nerves, cartilage and bones be healed." I asked again what she felt.

"It feels really warm."

"Cool. Let me try it again. Spirit of pain I command you to leave. Knee be healed right now."

"It's warmer now."

"Okay, one more time. Lord let's get this knee healed. Pain and inflammation I command you to leave in the name of Jesus." I asked again what she felt.

"It's really hot now."

While her knee was healing, I taught her about the battle. I told her to stand in faith and to command the symptoms to leave if they returned, the same way I did to make them go. She understood.

I saw Amy three weeks later and asked how her knee felt. She said it felt great. I asked if she was serious. With a smile, she looked at me and said, "Yeah—it feels great!"

When Amy wasn't healed, the easiest way to explain the lack of healing would be to assume that God didn't want her to be healed. The fact that she was healed later demonstrates that it wasn't a problem with God. It was a problem with her. Unfortunately, we often blame God when healing doesn't happen. But that should be the last explanation we consider.

The most likely explanation for failed healing is our own lack of faith. The next thing to consider is that some obstacle may be present in the life of the one we're praying with that needs to be removed. Sometimes it's a spirit of sickness; sometimes it's an attitude toward God that needs to change. Sometimes it's emotional trauma. In this case, it was fear. Once the fear was removed she was healed.

Healing is meant to draw people into a loving relationship with Jesus. Many times the thing that keeps them from experiencing healing is something like fear. Many people have been wounded by Christians. The fear that they have toward us creates a wall around their heart. The only way we'll ever be able to pray with them is if they take down the wall. The only way to get them take down the wall is by showing them love. Once we've shown them enough love to convince them we're safe, the wall around their heart can be taken down. Once the wall is down we can release the power of God. His power testifies to the truth of our message—that God loves them. The truth that God loves them sets them free.

As my friend Steve Harmon says, "Love takes down the wall. Power testifies to the truth. The truth sets them free."

THANK YOU FOR PURCHASING THIS BOOK

I HOPE YOU'VE BEEN ENCOURAGED by the book and I hope it inspires you to go out and release God's power and love.

The stories you've just read are the factual accounts of the miraculous things I've seen God do during the three years between 2008 and 2011.

I've got many more stories in my journal—written after 2011—that haven't been published in this volume. Another book (Volume 2) is in the works with plans to publish it in 2015.

Here's a sneak peek at a few of the titles from
My Craziest Adventures with God, Volume 2:

No More Shackles
The Three Monkeys
Time Warp
Tacos, Margaritas & Torn Biceps
Playing Chicken
Doomsday Preppers
… and more!

For more information
on healing & miracles,
visit my website:

PrayingMedic.com

To receive freebies, updates on my new book releases, and special offers, **sign up** in the sidebar at **PrayingMedic.com**. I don't sell or distribute your name or e-mail—I take your privacy seriously.

Also by Praying Medic

Divine Healing Made Simple
Simplifying the supernatural
to make healing and miracles
a part of your everyday life

To purchase in paperback:
http://bit.ly/Divine_Healing_Made_Simple_Paperback

To purchase the Kindle book:
http://bit.ly/Divine_Healing_Made_Simple_Kindle

Made in the USA
Middletown, DE
08 July 2016